Souk

Nadia Zerouali
& Merijn Tol

Souk
Feasting at the mezze table

Smith
Street
Books

Contents

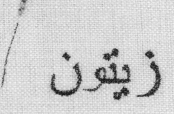

زيتون

Mezze

Imagine a summer Sunday afternoon. By the cool levees of the Berdawni River in Zahle, a provincial town in the Beka Valley in Lebanon, are beautiful tables set up in the shade. A large family begins Sunday lunch, an important family tradition. Everybody is there: Grandpa and Grandmother, Dad, Mum, the children, nephews, aunts and uncles. Soon there is no more space around the table. The carafe arrives filled with the famous aniseed liqueur *arak* ('lion's milk', named by the Zahliots, Zahle residents), together with fresh almonds and walnuts on ice and bowls of mixed nuts and pepitas (pumpkin seeds). The ingredients for these delights all come from the area, purchased at the local *souq*, or market. Not long after, bigger dishes are placed on the table — silky hummus and fried kibbeh balls, and big bowls of tabouleh or fattoush. Soon, the entire table is full. The whole ritual takes a couple of hours, and then you are completely full and can barely speak — especially any mezze novices, who overdo it almost immediately. The experts know how to pace themselves. The key? Don't eat too much bread. Then follow the meal with a small walk.

Mezze is not just the Middle Eastern equivalent of tapas; it is also a way of life. Throughout our time in the Middle East, it became clear to us that mezze is equal to the generosity and hospitality of the Levantine people. And when we think back, our hearts and minds fill with warmth and desire for the smells of the souq and those lovely hours spent around a mezze table full of sensational food. Fortunately, we can also fill our own table with our version of the mezze way of life. *Yalla!*

The culture of mezze

Mezzanic culture originated in the Ottoman Empire and can be found throughout the Levantine Mediterranean: Greece and Cyprus, Turkey (Hatay Province), Palestine, Jordan, Syria and Lebanon. But Lebanon is famous for having the richest, most untouched and sophisticated mezzanic culture. Mezze really took off in the 1920s in the town of Zahle, and today mezze restaurants still line either side of the Berdawni River. Lebanese people see this as the birthplace of mezze. Mezze is a real restaurant culture. It's not just about the food, but the whole experience — getting dressed up, going out, the location with a beautiful view, the food, the decor, the beautiful music. It's also all about seeing and being seen.

The different types of mezze are connected to the seasons and to the places where they are prepared and eaten. If you're by the sea you'll have fish dishes; if you're in the mountains, you'll find more meat. In summer there are fresh herbs and summer fruits and in winter there is *kashk* (fermented dairy) and canned vegetables. Traditionally, a lot of arak is poured (raki in Turkey or ouzo in Greece), to complement free-flowing conversation. Eating is a social event with lots of familiarity, laughter and chatter.

Traditionally, mezze culture only really existed in Arab Christian and Jewish circles. Fortunately, that's no longer the case, with the culture now being embraced by everyone. With or without arak. With friends or with family. Everything is possible.

Mezze?

According to some, the word *mezze* comes from the Arabic word *tamazzaza*, which means 'to taste in small bites'; in other words, taking the time to fully enjoy all of the smells, colours, aromas and flavours. It may also come from the Persian word *mazza* which means 'taste'. Or from the Turkish word *meza* for 'table' (*mesa* in Spanish and *mensa* in Latin).

Armenian influence

In Lebanon and Syria there is a large Armenian community that began with refugees in the early 20th century. Their kitchens are full of aromatic flavours such as paprika paste, pomegranate molasses, peppers, dried fruits, spicy sausages and stuffed vegetables, such as carrots. Armenians are very proud of their food culture (although it is said that Armenian cuisine in Armenia itself is different from that of the diaspora), and this has influenced cuisines in countries where they founded large communities. In these Armenian corners, the mezzanic culture has worked its way in. In Beirut (especially in the Armenian district of Bourj Hammoud) you will find famous Armenian mezze restaurants, such as Onno and Varouj, Mayrig and Badguèr, with their own Armenian mezze dishes, including spicy ma'anek sausages, grilled birds with pomegranate molasses, the Armenian version of tabouleh, borek and stuffed carrots, and kebabs with sour cherries.

The mezze table

Mezzanine tables are richly packed with dozens of cold and hot dishes, sometimes followed by a 'main course' of grilled meat, chicken or fish. The meal is always served with a glass of arak or, for the non-drinkers among us, there is, of course, a traditional Middle Eastern lemonade.

If you want to eat mezze like a real Arab, only eat with your right hand, using either three or four fingers, and with a piece of flatbread or sometimes a lettuce or cabbage leaf.

Our pantry

In recent years, cooking mezze in our kitchen has become much easier, thanks to so many Middle Eastern and Mediterranean ingredients, such as sumac, tahini and bulghur, being more readily available. Most of the ingredients in this book can be bought from the supermarket, but there are a few things you may have to seek out in a Turkish, Moroccan or Middle Eastern grocery store. And don't think you'll be buying jars or bottles of things that you'll use once and then never again — we constantly return to the same ingredients and we're sure you'll find them as delicious as we do. It's also just fun to go to these stores and look at all of the exciting and varied products they have. Sometimes we find dried apricots from Afghanistan, or those delicious bitter olives from the Middle East, or beautiful Syrian cookies, or white cheese shredded into strings.

The main thing we want to encourage is for you to be generous in your kitchen. Use many spices and herbs, which will bring lots of flavour. And trial, test and experiment! Use your own creativity and inspiration. Anything goes!

During our travels, we certainly noticed that the quality of the ingredients was far better than what we could get at home, so it's important to try to find good-quality herbs and spices. Ask your local Middle Eastern grocer what the best brands are.

— ADVIEH

An Iranian spice containing cinnamon, cardamom, cumin, rose petals, saffron and fennel. Delicious on red meat, chicken and rice dishes. Advieh is great to use as the base flavour of your dish, or you can just sprinkle some over to finish.

— ALLSPICE

Also known as pimento and myrtle pepper, allspice is the main ingredient in seven spice. It is a complex, hot spice that tastes like a combination of pepper, anise, nutmeg and cinnamon.

— ANISEED

A fragrant spice eaten in many cultures. We use it in both sweet and savoury dishes, and it's particularly good on labne.

— ARGAN OIL

Argan oil is nutty and fragrant. Good-quality oil is pressed by hand, which makes it quite expensive (but worth it). It's also comparatively rare, as the argan tree is only grown in the triangular piece of land between Essaouira, Agadir and Safi. This oil is great for dipping with some bread or for drizzling over soup, roasted vegetables or couscous.

— BAHARAT (MIDDLE EASTERN)

A spice mix made of cinnamon, cumin, coriander, chilli, pepper, clove and cardamom. It is delicious with chicken, rice, legumes and meat dishes.

— BAHARAT (TUNISIAN)

The Tunisian version is made of scented cinnamon and rose petals with a black pepper kick. It is delicious with grilled chicken, in tajines, couscous and stews, and on pumpkin (winter squash).

— BARBERRIES

Also known as berberis, these are tart berries, very popular in Iranian cuisine. We really love them – they have a deliciously fresh, aromatic and lightly acidic taste and texture. We fold them through bread dough and add them to rice, salads and meat and chicken dishes.

— CARDAMOM

A Middle Eastern staple spice, common in coffee and sweet and savoury dishes. Sometimes we use the whole pod and sometimes just the seeds.

— CORIANDER SEED AND CUMIN SEED

We use these two spices a lot. Together with cinnamon and seven spice, they are on our shopping list almost every week.

— COUSCOUS BERKOUKES

This is a variety of hand-rolled coarse couscous, traditionally made and dried in the open air. The robust structure of the couscous makes it extra delicious.

To prepare the couscous, mix it with a spoonful of oil and some salt, sprinkle some water over, then rub and steam the couscous for 10 minutes in the upper part of a couscous pan. Remove from the pan and gently fluff the grains. Repeat the steaming again for two more minutes. Season with some olive oil or butter and salt. If you don't have a couscous pan, you can boil the couscous for 10 minutes in stock or water, or in milk with sugar and cinnamon for a sweet version.

— DILL SEED

A surprisingly little-used spice. Dill seed is sweet and spicy, and very popular in the kitchens of Gaza.

— DRIED LEGUMES

If you have the time it's so much better to cook legumes yourself, rather than using the canned stuff, which is invariably mushy and can have sugar added. We make large portions at a time and store them soaked or cooked in the freezer.

— DRIED MINT

An absolutely classic pairing with dairy. The flavour of dried mint is very different to that of fresh mint. It gives dishes an undeniable Middle Eastern/Turkish flavour.

— DRIED ROSE BUDS

These are wonderful with red meat, chicken and vegetables, sprinkled on sweet or savoury yoghurt, and in lemonades, coffee, tea and cocktails.

— DUKKAH

Dukkah is originally an Egyptian blend of spices, nuts and roasted chickpeas. *Dukh* means 'to pound', and all the ingredients are – you guessed it – finely ground. In our homemade dukkah, we use many spices and herbs, such as cumin, aniseed, coriander and ginger, but also sesame and poppy seeds, almonds and roasted chickpeas. Delicious on labne, or just with some oil to dip, dukkah is also wonderful in salad dressings, sprinkled on baked, roasted and raw vegetables, and boiled or baked eggs.

— FILO PASTRY

If you can, try to use the long rolls you find at Turkish and Moroccan grocery stores. With filo you always have to work fast, sprinkle with oil and keep the pastry under a clean tea towel.

— FLATBREAD

When we say flatbread, we mean Lebanese flatbread — the flat, round bread in plastic bags found in Turkish and Moroccan grocery stores. You'll see that we bake a lot of bread in this book (nothing beats freshly baked bread and it always disappears very quickly!), but if you don't want to make your own, you can always replace it with flat Arabic bread or Lebanese flatbread. Most Turkish, Moroccan and Middle Eastern grocers will stock flatbread, and it should keep well in its bag for a couple of days. In the Middle East, flatbread is generally served in its bag on the table as it dries out quickly.

— FREEKEH

Freekeh is young-harvested green wheat that has been roasted, producing a light and smoky flavour. Freekeh is often eaten in the Middle East as a hot dish with lamb, almonds, spices and yoghurt, but its flavour is also great with raw or roasted vegetables, spices, fresh herbs, meat, fish, nuts … yes, pretty much everything! We are fans.

— HALOUMI, TULUM AND TURKISH WHITE CHEESE

Long gone are the days where we had to search for haloumi, as it's now available at the supermarket. Tulum cheese and Turkish white cheese, however, can still only be bought from Turkish or Middle Eastern grocers.

Tulum cheese is a fairly dry, salty goat's cheese, good for crumbling and ideal to have in your fridge. It's always delicious with baked eggs, in a salad or with vegetables, and it keeps very well for weeks. In Turkey they eat it as a snack with raki.

Turkish white cheese is similar to feta and can be made of cow, goat or sheep's milk (or a combination thereof).

— KATAIFI PASTRY

Kataifi is a kind of ultra-fine angel hair pastry that is actually very easy to use. Just mix with a little melted butter and sugar (if using for sweets) and then use as a base or topping. You'll find it at Turkish or Mediterranean grocers, usually in the freezer section.

— LIKAMA

A spice mix from Morocco that contains cumin, cinnamon, carrot, coriander, black and white pepper, aniseed and ginger powder. Delicious in tajines and couscous, and on grilled vegetables, lamb, chicken and beef.

— MAHLAB

The ground pits of mahlab cherries, the flavour is somewhere between bitter almond and cherry. Most commonly used in sweet dishes. We like to use it in puddings and ice cream.

— MASTIC

Dried resin from the mastic tree (part of the pistachio family), which grows mainly in Greece and the Middle East. It imparts a very unique flavour and texture, and is used in cookies, bread, ice cream and desserts, and in savoury dishes such as stews.

– MOGHRABIEH (PEARL COUSCOUS)

Moghrabieh originates from Lebanon and the Middle East, and the name means 'couscous of the Maghreb'. It is somewhere between couscous and pasta. Lebanese moghrabieh is made of semolina, water and salt, and is formed into beautiful pearl shapes. In the northern Lebanese city of Tripoli, moghrabieh is traditionally eaten with chickpeas and onions and sometimes chicken or other meat flavoured with pepper, cinnamon and caraway. We also find moghrabieh really great in salads and soups.

– NUTS AND SEEDS

Our kitchens are full of them. Pistachios, almonds, walnuts, pine nuts, sesame seeds – we use them a lot, in traditional recipes and in our own way.

– ORANGE-BLOSSOM WATER

Orange-blossom water or *mazaher* is the deliciously flavoured distillate of the bitter orange blossom. Orange-blossom water is used in sweet dishes (pastries, cakes and ice cream) and savoury dishes (tajines and dressings). But you can also add just a few drops to boiling water to make a drink known as 'white coffee' in the Middle East. The flavour is lovely, but it's also very good for digestion after a long dinner. Start with a few drops, because the taste is strong!

– OREGANO

Of course, of course, you know what oregano is, but we would like to recommend that you look out for fresh oregano with thick greyish leaves, which is more similar to *Oregano syriacum*, the oregano you find in the Middle East.

– POMEGRANATE MOLASSES

Pomegranate molasses (*dibs el rumman*) is made from boiling down the juice of sour and sweet pomegranates, which produces a beautiful, deep brown syrup. It's great on vegetables, grains and salads, in sauces and with meat or chicken. It's also delicious mixed with a little tahini.

– PRESERVED LEMON

An absolute must in Moroccan cuisine. You can buy them pre-made, but they're so simple to make yourself – just fragrant unsprayed lemons and sea salt. Preserved lemons make everything delicious. They're great with chicken, red meat, in soups, over labne, and also amazing thinly sliced in salads, dressings or sauces. They give a special kick, so experiment!

— RAS EL HANOUT

Ras el hanout means 'the head of the store' or 'top shelf'. No ras el hanout is the same, because everyone makes their own version. Ours has cumin, coriander, cinnamon, pepper, ginger, fennel seed, star anise, lavender, grains of paradise, clove, saffron and turmeric. Suitable for chicken and meat dishes, with roasted vegetables, in a broth for couscous, in tajines … almost everything!

— RAS EL HANOUT (SWEET)

We also make a sweet version of ras el hanout, containing cumin, fennel, aniseed, star anise, cardamom, cinnamon, ginger, grains of paradise, pepper, coriander and dried rose petals. We like to use this sweet spice mix in cakes, cookies, to give coffee or chocolate milk a spicy kick, or with sweet roasted vegetables such as pumpkin (winter squash) and carrot.

— RED PEPPER PASTE

Look for *tatli biber* and *aci biber* in Turkish grocery stores. We always use *tatli*, which is a sweet pepper paste. It's a great flavouring for salads, sauces and soups, and with kebabs or chicken.

— ROSEWATER

Rosewater is distilled from the petals of the Damascus rose. Rosewater is usually used in sweet preparations, such as syrups, jams, pastries, cookies and desserts. It's best to start with just a few drops, as the fragrance is strong and can easily become overpowering if you add too much.

— SAFFRON

A golden spice that imparts a beautiful warm colour and fragrance. We like to use it in rice dishes, and with chicken and fish and dairy. The better the quality, the better the flavour.

— SAHLEP

Powdered orchid root. In Turkey and Greece, *sahlep* is often used to prepare a cosy hot drink, sprinkled with chopped nuts. It's generally sold as a powder — try a few different ones, as some are very sweet.

— SEVEN SPICE

A spice mix from the Middle East, used in particular in Syria and Lebanon. Seven spice is indispensable in meat kibbeh, for preparing moghrabieh and in sauces and stews. We make ours with black pepper, allspice, cinnamon, coriander, ginger, white pepper, nutmeg and cloves.

— STAR ANISE

Spicier than aniseed and with a much stronger flavour — use sparingly!

— SUCUK

The Turkish dried garlic sausage, which is available at most Turkish grocery stores. Delicious with eggs, vegetables, soups … most things, really. We like to cook ours with a little sumac.

— SUMAC

Sumac is made from the ground berry of the sumac plant. It has a fresh, tart flavour and we use it liberally, as you might use pepper. It's classically used in the Middle Eastern fattoush salad, but it's also amazing with eggs, dairy, chicken, vegetables, sucuk sausage ... anything that could do with a little freshness.

— TABL

A North African spice mix made primarily of coriander, caraway, cumin, and chilli pepper. Tabl is essential for making harissa, but also delicious in chicken dishes or as marinade for fish and vegetables.

— TAHINI

This Middle Eastern ingredient is made from very finely ground unroasted sesame seeds. Tahini is a key ingredient in hummus, but it's also great as a dressing on salads, with roasted vegetables, meat, poultry and fish, or in ice cream and desserts. Try it as a dip for dried figs. A life without tahini is much less delicious!

— TAMARIND

You may know of tamarind as a paste or pulp, but in Middle Eastern cuisine, it's also used as a spice. We like to use tamarind with meat and chicken, in dressings and in sauces.

— TURKISH RED PEPPER FLAKES (PUL BIBER, ALEPPO PEPPER, ISOT PEPPER, PEPPERONCINO)

Each of these have subtle differences in heat and texture, but they're essentially all spicy red pepper flakes. *Pul biber* is Turkish and has a mild sweetness; Aleppo pepper is similar; isot pepper is smoked pepper; and *pepperoncino* is hot Italian pepper. We use them together to taste, in the same way that we use different textures and flavours of salt.

— TURMERIC

We have recently rediscovered turmeric, especially in its root form. And no, not because of the health claims, but because of its fantastic flavour and vibrant colour. Turmeric is widely used in Arabic cuisine, in both sweet and savoury dishes.

— VINE LEAVES

If you're using tinned leaves, try a few varieties to find one you like, as there is often a big difference in quality.

— YOGHURT

We prefer creamy, full-fat yoghurt. Turkish yoghurt is best, if you can find it, otherwise Greek-style yoghurt is the next best thing. When making labne, pot-set yoghurt will give you the best results.

— ZA'ATAR (LEBANESE)

An indispensable spice mix of ground dried marjoram (or oregano), sesame seeds, floral sumac and salt flakes for a lot of texture and taste. This mixture is a main ingredient of *man'ouche*, the Lebanese breakfast of fresh flatbread with olive oil and za'atar. It's also delicious with lamb, chicken and egg dishes, and on labne and roasted vegetables.

— ZA'ATAR (PALESTINIAN)

Our Palestinian za'atar is quite green in colour and varies from the Lebanese by using different herbs and a little olive oil. Palestinian za'atar is delicious as a dip with olive oil and fresh bread — a dish that's perfect for breakfast and makes us happy at any time of the day. We also find it tasty when sprinkled on labne or baked eggs, or in a flatbread sandwich, with cucumbers, tomatoes and sprigs of fresh mint.

Drinks and cocktails

With all the amazing ingredients available to us, such as sumac, oregano and pomegranate molasses, it's easy to make truly enchanting cocktails and lemonades ... It's also hard to stop at one glass!

— ARAK

Arak is an aniseed liqueur from the Middle East. It turns a beautiful milky colour when water is added, and it has a deliciously fresh aniseed flavour. If you can't find arak, Turkish raki and Greek ouzo are quite similar and make great substitutes.

— COCKTAILS AND LEMONADES

The cocktails in this chapter are wonderful to drink before dinner (traditionally, only arak is drunk at mealtimes). The fresh lemonades are a great non-alcoholic accompaniment to a mezze table.

Arak or raki

WITH FRESH ALMONDS AND WALNUTS

In Lebanon, when eating at local restaurants, we would often be served arak as an aperitif, commonly accompanied by fresh almonds in spring and fresh walnuts in summer.

— Soak fresh almonds or walnuts in hot water for a good 30 minutes. Drain and place the nuts in small bowls.

— Place the bottle of arak on the table, along with small liqueur glasses, carafes of cold water and small bowls of ice cubes. Pour the arak into glasses and top with water and ice to your liking. The traditional ratio is one-third arak and two-thirds water.

Arak

WITH LIMONCELLO, GRAPEFRUIT AND ORANGE-BLOSSOM WATER

— Pour a little arak into small glasses and add a small spoonful of limoncello. Top up with cold water, and adjust the flavours to your liking.

— Using a small, sharp knife, peel a few strips of zest from an organic grapefruit. Cut the flesh into segments, cutting between the pith. Divide the grapefruit segments among the glasses and garnish with the zest. Finally, add a little spoonful of orange-blossom water. Serve ice cold,

Arak aperitif
WITH FIG SYRUP

— *Makes 2 glasses*

2 DRIED FIGS *torn*

2 TABLESPOONS SUGAR

ORGANIC LEMON ZEST

ARAK *(or raki)*

Arak pairs wonderfully with figs — so this cocktail makes perfect sense! Because fig syrup is not easy to find, we make it ourselves. This drink is delicious in hot weather.

— Bring the figs, sugar, lemon zest and 250 ml (8½ fl oz/ 1 cup) water to the boil in a small saucepan. Let the figs gently bubble on low heat for 10–15 minutes until they are soft. Pour through a sieve, reserving the syrup. Set aside to cool, then chill.

— Pour some arak into glasses and add a little fig syrup to taste. Top with chilled water and add a generous amount of ice. If you like, garnish with more dried figs.

Lemon geranium lemonade

— *Makes about 1.5 litres (1½ qts) lemonade*

3 LEMONS

75 G (2½ OZ) SUGAR

2 LEMON GERANIUM SPRIGS
unsprayed

These thirst-quenchers prove that lemonade isn't just for children. The lemon geranium and the oregano gives these fresh lemonades a spicy, grown-up kick.

— Wash the lemons, halve them and place them in a large bowl. Add the sugar and the leaves from one geranium sprig. Using your hands, knead everything together for a few minutes, until all the juice has transferred into the sugar. Allow to sit for at least 30 minutes and up to a few hours. Pour through a sieve and reserve the syrup.

— Pour the syrup into a carafe, top up with about 1.5 litres (1½ qts) of ice-cold water and garnish with the remaining sprig of lemon geranium.

Oregano lemonade

— *Makes about 1.5 litres (1½ qts) lemonade*

3–4 OREGANO SPRIGS
(or thyme)

75 G (2½ OZ) SUGAR

3 LEMONS

— Remove the leaves from the oregano sprigs. Place them in a small food processor with the sugar and blitz. Wash the lemons, halve them and place them in a large bowl. Add the oregano sugar and, using your hands, knead everything together for a few minutes until all the juice has transferred into the sugar. Allow to sit for at least 30 minutes and up to a few hours. Pour through a sieve and reserve the syrup.

— Pour the syrup into a carafe, top up with about 1.5 litres (1½ qts) of chilled water and some ice cubes or crushed ice.

Pomegranate molasses lemonade
WITH SUMAC SYRUP

— *Makes about 1.5 litres
(1½ qts) lemonade*

1 LEMON

100 ML (3½ FL OZ) POMEGRANATE
  MOLASSES

2 TABLESPOONS SUMAC

2–4 TABLESPOONS SUGAR

1.5 LITRES (1½ QTS) CHILLED SODA
  WATER (CLUB SODA)

We are huge fans of pomegranate molasses, so it shouldn't be a surprise that we've included it in a drink. The fact that it's such a delicious drink surprised even us!

— Wash the lemon and finely grate the zest. Cut in half and squeeze the juice into a small saucepan. Add the zest, molasses, sumac, sugar to taste and a little boiling water. Bring to a simmer over low heat and reduce to a thick syrup. Set aside to cool.

— Pour the syrup into a carafe and top up with the soda water and some ice cubes or crushed ice.

Homemade ayran

WITH SUMAC AND CARDOMOM

— *Makes more than 1 litre (1 qt)*

500 G (1 LB 2 OZ) YOGHURT

500 ML (17 FL OZ/2 CUPS) MILK

PINCH OF SALT

SUMAC

3–4 CARDAMOM PODS
   lightly crushed

Ayran is a fresh-tasting, sour–sweet dairy drink that is popular in countries such as Turkey, Lebanon, Iran and Armenia. The Turks like to drink ayran when eating kebab and we really think this is the perfect combination, especially this version, which is flavoured with sumac and cardamom — a great counterbalance to the fatty meat. Add sumac and cardamom to your own taste.

— Whisk the yoghurt, milk and salt until foamy. Add a little water if you want the consistency a bit thinner.

— Whisk in as much sumac as you like (we add a full tablespoon, but you might want to start with less). Add the cardamom pods and set aside for 30 minutes to infuse. Remove the cardamom pods, whisk again until frothy and serve cold in tall glasses.

Ginger beer

WITH ORANGE AND ORANGE-BLOSSOM WATER

— *Makes 1 litre (1 qt)*

3–4 CM (2¼–2½ IN) PIECE GINGER
  grated

200 G (7 OZ) SUGAR

1 TEASPOON TARTARIC ACID

JUICE OF 2 LEMONS

½ TEASPOON DRIED YEAST

GRATED ZEST OF ½ ORANGE

ORANGE-BLOSSOM WATER

Who would have thought it was so easy to make your own ginger beer? Ginger with orange and a hint of orange-blossom is such a fantastic combination. This is brilliant with gin, or drink it as is with some ice.

— Combine the ginger with the sugar, tartaric acid, lemon juice and 200 ml (7 fl oz) water in a saucepan and bring to a simmer over low heat. Allow it to cook to a light syrup. Add the yeast and about 1 litre (1 qt) of lukewarm water and stir. Transfer to a 2 litre (2 qt) plastic bottle and place the cap on, but do not tighten — leave it slightly loose so gas can escape. Set aside in a warm, dark place for 2–3 days. Check a few times a day and release the cap to allow gas to escape.

— Strain the liquid through a sieve into a clean bottle, then stir in the orange zest and add orange-blossom water to taste. Keep the ginger beer in the fridge until you're ready to drink it.

Sour cherry juice

WITH ROSEWATER

— *Makes 1 litre (1 qt)*

1 LITRE (1 QT) SOUR CHERRY JUICE

ROSEWATER

LEMON JUICE *(optional)*

Sour cherry juice hasn't hit the mainstream yet, but we think it's only a matter of time. For now, you have to go to a Middle Eastern grocer or deli for a bottle of this divine juice. If you can't find any, replace it with unsweetened pomegranate or grape juice and add some lemon juice.

— Flavour the cherry juice with some rosewater: start with a few drops and add more to taste. Too sweet or not sour enough? Then add some lemon juice to taste. Leave the juice in the fridge to chill before serving.

Absinthe cocktail
WITH OREGANO

— *Makes 2*

CRUSHED ICE

60 ML (2 FL OZ/¼ CUP) ABSINTHE

60 ML (2 FL OZ/¼ CUP) LIME JUICE

60 ML (2 FL OZ/¼ CUP) SUGAR SYRUP

250 ML (8½ FL OZ/1 CUP) ICE-COLD
  WATER

CUCUMBER SLICES

2 OREGANO SPRIGS *(or thyme)*

Absinthe, with its famous reputation, shares an aniseed flavour with arak. This is a variation on the classic Green Fairy cocktail: the oregano gives it a spicy depth and makes it the ideal drink before dinner. For a simple sugar syrup, bring 200 g (7 oz) of sugar and 240 ml (8 fl oz) water to the boil and heat until the sugar has melted. Cool well. Store the sugar syrup in a dark place in a sealed bottle.

— Chill two highball glasses in advance. Place some crushed ice in a cocktail shaker and add the absinthe, lime juice, sugar syrup and water. Shake for a few seconds. Divide the cocktail between the glasses. Garnish with slices of cucumber and a sprig of oregano. Add ice if you like.

Rose–barberry gin

WITH ROSEMARY AND ORANGE

— *Makes 700 ml (23½ fl oz) gin*

700 ML (23½ FL OZ) GIN

2 TABLESPOONS BARBERRIES

2 TABLESPOONS DRIED ROSEBUDS

PEEL OF ½ ORANGE

1 SPRIG ROSEMARY

Of course, a good gin is already good, with its small hint of juniper berry. But sometimes you just want an extra hit of Arabic spices. So, try infusing your gin with different flavours. We think this is a good place to start, but if you prefer to use other aromatics, be our guest!

— Pour the gin into an airtight bottle, add the barberries, rosebuds, orange peel and rosemary, and seal. Place the bottle in a cool, dark place to infuse for a few days, shaking the bottle several times a day. Test whether the gin is to your taste. If it has infused enough, strain the gin back into its original bottle or into another sealed bottle. Serve the gin straight or with some ice and/or iced water.

Cold mezze

Mezze menus in restaurants are often so long and extensive they could be mistaken for books! There is a lot to choose from, both cold and hot dishes. Our cold mezze consists of a mixture of traditional dishes such as hummus, moutabal (eggplant spread), fattoush salad and tabouleh, plus our own creative interpretations of the mezze table. Take, for example, our labne variations. Labne (strained yoghurt) is usually just served with some olive oil and/or some garlic on the mezze table, but we wanted to pair this ingredient with different tasty flavours, such as sumac, oregano, pomegranate seeds, lemon zest and so on. It turned out to be a big hit and showcased our approach to making creative mezze: having respect for the tradition and using ingredients sourced from their region of origin. What's even better is that you can serve them all together. Look at the following recipes as a menu, and choose what you want.

فجل

Lebanese hummus
WITH BUTTER AND PINE NUTS

— *Serves 4–6*

300 G (10½ OZ) DRIED CHICKPEAS
    (GARBANZO BEANS) *soaked for a few*
    hours with a pinch of baking powder

½ TEASPOON BAKING POWDER

WHITE TAHINI

¼ GARLIC CLOVE

LEMON JUICE

SALT

50 G (1¾ OZ) BUTTER

SMALL HANDFUL OF PINE NUTS

Everybody now knows and loves hummus. Its popularity has gone sky-high in recent years. But ... there is hummus and there is hummus. We are happy to admit that we are strict hummus police. We've been fighting the fight for a while, but our task is not yet done. More and more people are making their own hummus (instead of the usually terrible ready-made stuff) but it is a refined craft. It takes a lot of attention and love, and the best ingredients. We start with the most delicious dried chickpeas (usually Spanish), the best white tahini (usually our own) and organic lemons. In the Middle East, most families have special food processors with slim, sharp blades just for making hummus. In our food processor, we have one special blade that we use only for hummus. We process the mixture for a very long time, stopping and testing and adjusting very regularly. Along with tahini, lemon juice and salt, add as much water as you need to make your hummus silky and pale. Only when you think it's perfect is it done. Fine tune and fine-tune. Anyone who thinks making hummus is easy is wrong!

— Boil the chickpeas and baking powder in fresh water until you can squash them between your index finger and thumb. Let them drain well and cool a little. Place the chickpeas in a food processor with a good spoon of tahini, the garlic, some lemon juice, salt and a splash of water. Keep processing the mixture, testing, and fine-tuning it as you go.

— The hummus is ready when it is perfectly silky and well flavoured. Transfer it to a serving dish and make some trenches in the surface. Heat the butter with the pine nuts in a small frying pan over medium heat and cook until the nuts are golden. Pour the warm butter with pine nuts over the hummus and serve.

Moutabal

EGGPLANT SPREAD WITH YOGHURT,
POMEGRANATE AND OREGANO

— *Serves 4–6*

2 EGGPLANTS (AUBERGINES)

¼ GARLIC CLOVE

2–3 TABLESPOONS FULL-FAT
   YOGHURT

SALT

OLIVE OIL

SMALL HANDFUL POMEGRANATE
   SEEDS

SMALL HANDFUL OREGANO LEAVES

Moutabal may seem simple to make, but the secret to this dish is to start with excellent produce. Good eggplants (aubergines) make good moutabal.

— Roast the eggplants directly on the flame of a gas cooker until they are blackened and very soft. If you do not have a gas cooker, you can grill them on a barbecue or under a hot grill (broiler), although the tasty smoked flavour may not be the same. Let the eggplants cool slightly. Rinse them gently, scraping off all of the blackened skin, but don't wash them too thoroughly, otherwise you will lose your flavour. Purée the eggplant with the garlic and yoghurt, adding a little more yoghurt to taste, if desired. Season with salt.

— Transfer the moutabal to a bowl, drizzle with olive oil and scatter over the pomegranate seeds and oregano leaves.

Fattoush

SALAD WITH CUCUMBER, TOMATO, HERBS, POMEGRANATE AND SUMAC

— *Serves 4—6*

4 LEBANESE CUCUMBERS

8 SMALL TOMATOES

SPRIGS OF MINT, OREGANO,
   TARRAGON, PARSLEY,
   BASIL AND DILL

2–3 LITTLE GEM LETTUCES

3 FLATBREADS *torn*

OLIVE OIL

SALT

SUMAC

100 ML (3½ FL OZ) POMEGRANATE
   MOLASSES

1 GARLIC CLOVE *finely chopped*

LEMON JUICE

Together with tabouleh, fattoush is a classic Lebanese mezze salad. You can choose to serve one or the other, or both. Traditionally, it is a salad of cucumber, tomato, crispy bread, herbs, pomegranate molasses and sumac. We have honoured the traditional recipe, but we also like to add the best herbs we have in generous quantities: tarragon, oregano, mint, even basil ... You do not have to hold back!

— Halve the cucumbers lengthways and slice them on the diagonal. Cut the tomatoes into quarters. Pick the leaves from the herbs and cut the lettuce into strips.

— Mix the torn flatbread with some oil, salt and a sprinkling of sumac and cook under the grill (broiler) until golden brown and crisp.

— Mix the pomegranate molasses with 200 ml (7 fl oz) of olive oil, the garlic, 1 tablespoon sumac, some lemon juice and salt to taste.

— In a salad bowl, combine the vegetables and herbs with your hands. Just before serving, add the bread, drizzle with the dressing and toss so that everything is nice and coated.

— For a quick variation, simply sprinkle the salad with some olive oil, salt and pomegranate molasses.

What makes a great mezze spread? We've learned that a traditional meal should always begin with a bowl of tabouleh or fattoush, with some labne and shankleesh to accompany. Of course, a piece of flatbread or a nice lettuce or white cabbage leaf is indispensable as cutlery.

Classic tabouleh

— *Serves 4–6*

2 RIPE TOMATOES

2 TABLESPOONS FINE BULGHUR

2 BUNCHES PARSLEY

½ BUNCH MINT

3 SPRING ONIONS (SCALLIONS)

½ GREEN CHILLI

SALT AND PEPPER

SEVEN SPICE

2 LEMONS

125 ML (4 FL OZ/½ CUP) OLIVE OIL

A classic tabouleh, in accordance with the ten commandments of our friend Kamal Mouzawak, Lebanese chef and restaurateur.

— Wash the tomatoes, cut them into small cubes and put them in a large salad bowl. Mix in the bulghur so that the grain can soak up the juices from the tomato.

— Pick the parsley into little sprigs, removing most of the stalk. Pick the mint leaves and wash well along with the parsley and spring onions. Pat them dry.

— Very finely chop the spring onions and green chilli, then rub with some salt and pepper and add a pinch of seven spice. Add to the salad bowl, but do not mix. Chop the parsley and mint very well and add to the bowl. Halve the lemons and squeeze the juice over the salad. Mix well just before serving and adjust the flavour with the olive oil, and a little more lemon juice, salt and seven spice, if needed. The tabouleh should be juicy and fresh, but not swimming in liquid. And most importantly, serve immediately – tabouleh should not be kept waiting ...

Classic shankleesh

— *Serves 4–6*

200 G (7 OZ) CRUMBLED TULUM
   CHEESE WITH NIGELLA SEEDS
   (available from Turkish delis)
2 WHITE ONIONS
2 RIPE TOMATOES
1 BUNCH PARSLEY
100 ML (3½ FL OZ) OLIVE OIL

Real shankleesh cheese can unfortunately be difficult to obtain. To make things easier, we have replaced this typically fermented, creamy ripe cheese with Turkish tulum cheese with nigella seeds.

— Crumble the cheese and place onto individual plates or one larger serving dish. Peel the onions and cut them into cubes. Wash the tomatoes and cut them into cubes. Wash and dry the parsley and pick the leaves. Divide the parsley leaves, onion and tomato among the plates or arrange on the serving dish. Mix all the ingredients together and drizzle with a generous amount of olive oil.

Classic labne

— *Serves 4–6*

2 TEASPOONS SALT *plus extra*
500 G (1 LB 2 OZ/2 CUPS)
   YOGHURT *(preferably thick
   Turkish yoghurt)*
EXTRA-VIRGIN OLIVE OIL

Labne (strained yoghurt) is eaten for breakfast and as mezze in the Middle East, and is generally just served drizzled with a little olive oil. You can see our inventive take on page 67. Like hummus, labne should be scooped up with a piece of flatbread, straight into the mouth. No mess, no fuss.

— Stir the salt through the yoghurt. Place a square of clean muslin (cheesecloth) on your work surface and spoon the yoghurt on top. Tie up the corners to create a bag, then transfer to a colander set over a bowl or saucepan. Place in the fridge and leave for at least 4 hours (for soft labne) or overnight (for firm labne), making sure the yoghurt doesn't touch the drained whey. Spread the yoghurt over a flat dish or plate, then sprinkle with some salt flakes. Drizzle generously with extra-virgin olive oil and serve.

Waraq einab

VINE LEAVES FILLED WITH LAMB MINCE AND RICE

— *Serves 4–6*

200 G (7 OZ) SHORT-GRAIN RICE
(such as arborio or Turkish rice)

2 TEASPOONS SEVEN SPICE

3 ONIONS *1 grated, 2 halved*

100 G (3½ OZ) MINCED (GROUND)
LAMB *(not too lean)*

2 TABLESPOONS TOMATO PASTE
(CONCENTRATED PURÉE)

SALT

VINE LEAVES *rinsed very well
and patted dry*

4 LAMB CHOPS

1 CINNAMON STICK

4 GARLIC CLOVES *halved*

FRESH BAY LEAVES

2 TOMATOES *halved*

OLIVE OIL

The Arabic *einab* means 'grape' and *waraq* means 'paper', so the name of this dish means 'grape paper'! The leaves are rolled up, as tight and as thin as possible. The thinner cigar shape is much better texturally, so it's worth the effort — as is the long, gentle simmer, which yields lovely, tender vine leaves. This version contains meat, but you can also use a filling of rice, tomato, sumac, seven spice, parsley and spring onion. While rolling, we do what the ladies in the Middle East do: gossip or talk about life. These are even more delicious the next day.

— In a wide bowl, combine the rice, seven spice, grated onion, lamb mince, tomato paste and a little salt and knead well. Lay a vine leaf in front of you and place a teaspoon of filling in a line across the centre of the leaf. Fold the left and right sides of the leaf inwards and, starting from the bottom, roll up as tightly as possible — just like a sleeping bag! Repeat until you've used up all of the filling.

— Place the lamb chops in a large frying pan and add the rolled vine leaves in a circle over the top. Add the cinnamon stick, garlic and bay leaves and finish with the halved onions and tomatoes. Add enough water to cover everything, then add a little salt and a spoon of olive oil. Sit a saucepan on top, which helps keep everything in place. Bring to a gentle simmer and cook for 45–60 minutes, until the vine leaves are soft and well cooked, adding a little extra hot water if the mixture gets dry. Serve lukewarm or cool, on the same day or, even better, 1–2 days later.

Mashed potato

WITH GARLIC AND BASIL

— *Serves 4–6*

4 LARGE YELLOW POTATOES

SALT

200 ML (7 FL OZ) MILD-TASTING
   OLIVE OIL

8 LARGE GARLIC CLOVES

1 BUNCH BASIL *leaves picked*

FLATBREADS *to serve*

We served this dish at one of Lebanon's most famous mezze restaurants: Casino Mhanna on the Berdawni River in Zahle. It's hard to believe that mashed potatoes without butter or milk can be this tasty!

— Peel the potatoes and roughly chop them into pieces. Put the potato in a saucepan, cover with cold water and season with salt, and bring to the boil. Cook for about 25 minutes, or until tender. In a food processor, purée the potatoes with a large spoonful of oil and some extra salt, if needed. Purée until smooth but firm.

— Meanwhile, heat the remaining oil in a frying pan. Add the garlic cloves and sauté until light brown. Remove from the heat, discard the garlic cloves and set the oil aside to cool slightly.

— Spoon the potato onto a serving plate. Top with basil leaves and drizzle generously with the garlic oil. Serve with flatbread.

We have created so many types of labne that we have lost count. It started in our first cookbook, and since then we've become obsessed. This is not at all traditional: in the Middle East they find our style of dressed labne highly exotic (albeit delicious!). Classically, labne is simply eaten with a spoon of olive oil and maybe a sprig of mint.

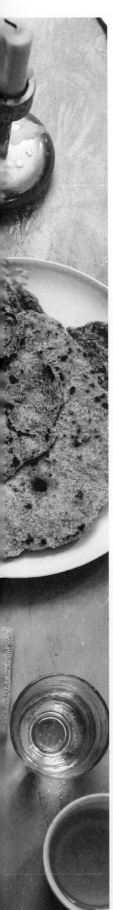

Labne
WITH POMEGRANATE SEEDS

— *Serves 6—8*

1 TABLESPOON SALT

1 KG (2 LB 3 OZ) THICK YOGHURT

2 TABLESPOONS SHELLED PISTACHIOS

3 OREGANO SPRIGS

½ POMEGRANATE *broken open*

1 TEASPOON ANISEED

POMEGRANATE MOLASSES

— Stir the salt through the yoghurt. Place a square of clean muslin (cheesecloth) on your work surface and spoon the yoghurt on top. Tie up the corners to create a bag, then transfer to a colander set over a bowl or saucepan. Transfer to the fridge and leave for at least 4 hours (for soft labne) or overnight (for firm labne), making sure the yoghurt doesn't touch the drained whey.

— Toast the pistachios until fragrant, then coarsely chop them. Pick the oregano leaves and separate the pomegranate seeds from the skin. Toast the aniseed if you like.

— Spread the labne over a serving plate and make some ridges in the surface using a circular motion. Scatter over the pistachios, oregano leaves, pomegranate seeds and aniseed, and drizzle with a spoonful of pomegranate molasses.

Labne
WITH CORIANDER AND TOMATO

— *Serves 6—8*

1 TABLESPOON SALT

1 KG (2 LB 3 OZ) THICK YOGHURT

3 TABLESPOONS ALMONDS

½ GREEN CHILLI

3 CORIANDER (CILANTRO) SPRIGS

¼ PRESERVED LEMON

1 TEASPOON CORIANDER SEEDS

1 RIPE TOMATO

EXTRA-VIRGIN OLIVE OIL

— Stir the salt through the yoghurt. Place a square of clean muslin (cheesecloth) on your work surface and spoon the yoghurt on top. Tie up the corners to create a bag, then transfer to a colander set over a bowl or saucepan. Transfer to the fridge and leave for at least 4 hours (for soft labne) or overnight (for firm labne), making sure the yoghurt doesn't touch the drained whey.

— If you like, toast the almonds until golden brown, then coarsely chop them. Finely chop the chilli, coriander and preserved lemon. Toast the coriander seeds if desired.

— Spread the labne over a serving plate and make some ridges in the surface using a circular motion. Halve the tomato and squeeze the seeds over the labne (use the rest of the tomato in a soup or salsa). Scatter over the almonds, chilli, coriander, preserved lemon and coriander seeds, and drizzle generously with olive oil.

A couple of years ago, I was walking through an old market in Jerusalem where I discovered hummus being made in the traditional Palestinian style. An old man was busy at a high wooden bowl working parsley, garlic and lemon juice with a wooden pestle. Then came the boiled chickpeas (garbanzo beans) and fragrant freshly ground tahini from a few doors up. At his hands it became a divine light green hummus, served for breakfast with pickled vegetables and fresh bread.

This hummus became an addiction for both of us and a classic on our mezze menu. The parsley gives the hummus a really fresh flavour.

Jerusalem hummus
WITH HARISSA

— *Serves 4–6*

250 G (9 OZ) DRIED CHICKPEAS
   (GARBANZO BEANS)
2½ TEASPOONS BAKING POWDER
½ BUNCH PARSLEY *plus extra to serve*
100 ML (3½ FL OZ) WHITE TAHINI
ABOUT 2 TABLESPOONS LEMON JUICE
1 GARLIC CLOVE
SALT
125 ML (4 FL OZ/½ CUP) HARISSA
EXTRA-VIRGIN OLIVE OIL
PITA BREADS OR FLATBREADS
   to serve

— In a large bowl, soak the chickpeas in plenty of cold water and 2 teaspoons of the baking powder for 12 hours or overnight. Rinse the chickpeas and drain well.

— Put the soaked chickpeas in a large saucepan and pour in enough cold water to cover by about 2 cm (¾ in). Add the remaining baking powder and bring to the boil. Cook the chickpeas with the lid half on the pan, skimming off any rising foam with a ladle. Boil the chickpeas for 2–3 hours, until they are very soft and cooked through. Drain well and set aside to cool completely.

— In a food processor, purée the parsley with about 100 ml (3½ fl oz) water and set aside. Purée the chickpeas with two-thirds of the tahini, as well as the lemon juice, garlic and some salt. With the processor running, add some of the parsley water; the hummus must be smooth and pale. Add more tahini, parsley water, lemon juice and/or salt, to taste.

— Spread the hummus over the bottom of a flat dish. Mix the harissa with a little oil and spoon over the hummus. Drizzle well with olive oil. Finely chop some extra parsley and sprinkle over the top. Serve with fresh pita bread or flatbread.

Wild fattoush

SALAD WITH PICKLED VEG, LABNE,
SUMAC BREAD, HERBS AND
POMEGRANATE MOLASSES

— *Serves 2–4*

500 ML (17 FL OZ/2 CUPS) APPLE
   CIDER VINEGAR

3 TABLESPOONS SALT *plus extra*

1 TABLESPOON DILL SEEDS

2–3 TABLESPOONS BEETROOT
   (BEET) JUICE

3 CARROTS *sliced*

3 TURNIPS *sliced*

1 BUNCH RADISHES *sliced*

250 G (9 OZ) WHOLEMEAL
   (WHOLEWHEAT) SPELT FLOUR

1 TEASPOON DRIED YEAST

1 TABLESPOON SUMAC

2 GARLIC CLOVES *grated*

OLIVE OIL

3 BABY GEM LETTUCES

FRESH HERBS *such as parsley,*
   basil, dill, mint, oregano,
   leaves picked

LABNE BALLS
   (see page 82)

POMEGRANATE MOLASSES

This wild fattoush is even more tangy than the original version. Instead of tomato and cucumber, our quick-pickled carrot, turnip and radish is delicious. And we also wanted to add the labne balls, just because cheese is especially tasty in a salad with crispy, garlicky bread. You can of course also let your imagination run free: the dough is great with lemon zest or dried oregano — you name it!

— Combine the apple cider vinegar, salt, dill seeds and beetroot juice with 500 ml (17 fl oz/2 cups) water in a saucepan and bring to the boil.

— Combine the carrot, turnip and radish in a saucepan or large heatproof bowl and pour the hot pickling liquid over the top. Leave for at least 30 minutes (the vegetables can pickle for as long as you like).

— Sift the spelt flour into a large bowl. Mix the yeast with some lukewarm water and leave the mixture to stand for 10 minutes until frothy. Mix the yeast mixture with the flour and add (little by little) as much extra lukewarm water to make a cohesive, smooth dough. Add a sprinkling of salt, the sumac and grated garlic, plus a spoon of olive oil. Knead the dough on your work surface for 10–15 minutes until smooth and velvety. Return the dough to the bowl, cover with a clean tea towel and leave in a warm place for 15–30 minutes. Knead it once more and divide into smaller, evenly sized pieces of dough. On a well-floured work surface, roll them out into thin discs. Cook each flatbread for a few minutes on a hot griddle or in a dry cast-iron frying pan, or even just under the grill (broiler) in a hot oven. It's quick: a few seconds on one side and then turn over. Let the breads cool and tear into pieces. If you have too many for the salad, just keep the extras and eat them with some hummus or labne.

— Cut the lettuce into strips, mix it with the fresh herbs and as much of the pickled vegetables as you like. Crumble the labne balls over the top and mix in the bread. Drizzle with olive oil and pomegranate molasses and season to taste.

This spicy dish was inspired by a delicious, hip and musical dinner party at The Palomar in London.

Mixed peppers
WITH ZA'ATAR FLATBREAD

— *Serves 6–8*

500 ML (17 FL OZ/2 CUPS) WHITE
    VINEGAR
2 TABLESPOONS SALT *plus extra*
500 G (1 LB 2 OZ) MIXED TURKISH
    GREEN PEPPERS
8 RED CHILLIES
6 GREEN CHILLIES
2 SPRING ONIONS (SCALLIONS)
3 GARLIC CLOVES
OIL *for frying*
SALT
EXTRA-VIRGIN OLIVE OIL
100 ML (3½ FL OZ) HARISSA

— Put the vinegar and salt in a saucepan with 500 ml (17 fl oz/ 2 cups) water and bring to the boil. Wash and dry the Turkish peppers. Set one pepper aside and cut the remaining peppers into coarse pieces. Place them in a clean saucepan, pour the hot vinegar mixture over the top and cover with a lid. Set aside to cool. The peppers will be delicious after a couple of hours, but they will taste even better if you store them in a sterilised airtight jar in a cool dark place for a few weeks.

— Peel the peppers with a fork. Preheat a grill (broiler) or barbecue.

— Roast 2 red chillies, 1 green chilli, the reserved Turkish pepper, spring onions and garlic under the hot grill or on the barbecue until the skins are blackened. Set aside to cool.

— Meanwhile, heat a little oil for frying and fry the rest of the chillies. Beware of spitting oil! Let them drain on paper towel and sprinkle with some salt. Remove the blackened skins from the grilled chillies, pepper, spring onion and garlic and purée the flesh using a mortar and pestle or a stick blender. Season with some olive oil and salt.

— Serve the pickled peppers and fried chillies with the chilli purée, harissa and za'atar flatbread.

Za'atar flatbread

— *Serves 6–8*

500 G (1 LB 2 OZ) WHOLEMEAL
    (WHOLEWHEAT) SPELT FLOUR
2 TEASPOONS DRIED YEAST
4 TABLESPOONS ZA'ATAR
2 TABLESPOONS OLIVE OIL
2 TEASPOONS SALT

— Mix the flour, yeast and za'atar in a large bowl. Make a well in the middle, pour in the oil and sprinkle over the salt. Add about 300 ml (10 fl oz) lukewarm water, little by little, kneading it by hand or in an electric mixer, until it comes together into a smooth dough. Leave covered under a clean cloth for 30 minutes. Shape into small, flat-tish rolls of dough and set aside to rest.

— Preheat the oven to 220°C (440°F). Bake the rolls on a baking tray placed in the middle of the oven for about 20 minutes, until cooked through and light brown. Serve immediately.

Crudites

WITH POMEGRANATE SUMAC DIP AND TARATOR SAUCE

— *Serves 6–8*

2–3 FIRM FENNEL BULBS

2–3 FIRM TURNIPS

2–3 FIRM CUCUMBERS

1 BUNCH RADISHES

200 G (7 OZ) TURKISH YOGHURT

3 TABLESPOONS POMEGRANATE
   MOLASSES

1 TABLESPOON SUMAC

SALT

1 GARLIC CLOVE

165 ML (5½ FL OZ) LEMON JUICE

200 ML (7 FL OZ) TAHINI

¼ BUNCH PARSLEY

No mezze table is complete without raw food. Traditionally, a large bowl of crisp fresh lettuce leaves, spring onions (scallions), hot green chillies, spicy radishes, small cucumbers and ripe tomatoes is served, sometimes with ice cubes in between the layers to keep everything crisp.

— Wash the vegetables well and cut them into pieces, slices and/or strips.

— To make the sumac dip, place the yoghurt in a bowl and stir in the pomegranate molasses, sumac and a pinch of salt.

— To make the tarator sauce, peel the garlic clove and grate it into a bowl. Add the lemon juice, then stir in the tahini and 80 ml (2½ fl oz) cold water. Stir until the mixture has a lovely mayonnaise-like consistency. Too thick? Add some extra water. Too thin? Add some more tahini. Finely chop the parsley. Season the tarator to taste with salt, then stir in the parsley.

— Serve the raw vegetables on a serving platter with the dip and the sauce in separate bowls.

Muhammara
WITH RAINBOW CHARD AND ONIONS

— *Serves 4–6*

2 TURKISH RED PEPPERS
   (*or large mild long red chillies*)
3 TABLESPOONS SWEET TURKISH RED
   PEPPER PASTE (*biber salçasi*)
3 GARLIC CLOVES
100 G (3½ OZ) WALNUTS
1 TABLESPOON CUMIN SEEDS
ABOUT 100 ML (3½ FL OZ)
   POMEGRANATE MOLASSES
SALT
OLIVE OIL
2–3 ONIONS *halved and sliced*
1 BUNCH RAINBOW CHARD
1 BUNCH DILL

The word *muhammara* comes from the Arabic word for 'red', *hamra*, and that's exactly what this dish is. The combination of rainbow chard and fried onions is magically delicious. Oh, and muhammara is also lovely with the kibbeh on page 89.

— Roast the peppers on a barbecue grill or over a gas flame until they are soft. Peel them and remove the seeds. Chop the peppers and combine with the pepper paste.

— Slice one of the garlic cloves. In a dry frying pan, toast the garlic with the walnuts and cumin seeds until light golden. Shake everything out of the pan and chop well. Mix three-quarters of the walnut mixture with the pepper paste and season with the pomegranate molasses and as much salt and olive oil as you like. Place in a serving dish and top with the remaining walnut mixture.

— Heat some olive oil in a deep frying pan over medium heat. Add the onion and and cook until golden brown (this takes a while and you have to keep stirring). Chop the rainbow chard and dill coarsely. Heat a little oil in a frying pan, add the remaining garlic cloves and cook the rainbow chard briefly until wilted. Add salt to taste. Place the rainbow chard in a dish and top with the fried onions.

Labne balls
WITH GARLIC AND NIGELLA SEEDS

— *Makes about 500 g*
(1 lb 2 oz)

SALT

1 KG (2 LB 3 OZ) ORGANIC FULL-
FAT GOAT'S YOGHURT

GARLIC *sliced*

NIGELLA SEEDS

OLIVE OIL

While it may not seem classy to eat labne balls with crackers, the ones on the page opposite are a totally different story. The spices work beautifully with labne, and they're ready in no time. We always have flour and semolina in our pantry, so they are perfect when you need something at the last minute!

— Mix a large pinch of salt into the yoghurt — it should be nice and salty. Spoon the yoghurt onto a clean square of muslin (cheesecloth) or tea towel, and place this into a sieve set over a bowl. Place in the fridge and leave to strain for two days, until you have firm labne.

— Fry the garlic in a little olive oil until golden brown. Set aside to cool.

— Scoop the labne out of the muslin and roll into balls using damp hands. Roll the balls in nigella seeds, then place in a clean jar. Add the fried garlic and top up the jar with olive oil. You can store in the fridge, or even in the pantry, because almost all of the moisture has been removed. Enjoy with a salad or with the crackers on the opposite page.

Quick crackers
WITH RAS EL HANOUT, DILL SEEDS AND SALT FLAKES

— *For 1 mezze table*

300 G (10 OZ) FLOUR *plus extra*

150 G (5½ OZ) SEMOLINA

80 ML (2½ FL OZ/⅓ CUP) OLIVE OIL

1 TABLESPOON RAS EL HANOUT

SALT FLAKES

DILL SEEDS

— Preheat the oven to 200°C (400°F). Line a baking tray with baking paper.

— In a mixing bowl, combine the flour, semolina, olive oil, ras el hanout, a little salt and as much lukewarm water as you need to make a soft dough. On a well-floured work surface, roll the dough out to about 2 mm (⅛ in) thick. Sprinkle with dill seeds, pressing the seeds into the dough, and then with salt flakes. Cut into strips and place on the baking tray. Bake the crackers in the oven for 10–15 minutes until golden brown.

Salad of ripe olives

WITH LEMON AND OREGANO

— *Serves 4–6*

150 G (5½ OZ) BLACK OLIVES

1 LEMON

1 SMALL BUNCH OREGANO

80 ML (2½ FL OZ/⅓ CUP)
   POMEGRANATE MOLASSES

2 TABLESPOONS EXTRA-VIRGIN
   OLIVE OIL

SALT

In Saida, Lebanon, we found the most beautifully displayed shiny black olives from Syria. Of course, we bought a kilo of them to take home. A friend of ours, who comes from the pomegranate-growing region of Turkey, suggested the addition of a generous amount of pomegranate molasses. The salty and sweet flavours are a brilliant combination!

— Place the olives in a bowl. Cut the lemon (peel and all) into small pieces and pick the oregano leaves. Add to the bowl with the olives. Mix just before serving, adding the pomegranate molasses, olive oil and salt to taste.

Salad of sumac onions

WITH OLIVE OIL DRESSING

— *Serves 4–6*

2 WHITE ONIONS

2 TABLESPOONS SUMAC

SALT

½ GARLIC CLOVE *finely chopped*

60 ML (2 FL OZ/¼ CUP) LEMON JUICE

180 ML (6 FL OZ) OLIVE OIL

100 G (3½ OZ) PEPPERY GREENS
   *(such as rocket/arugula, mustard
   greens or watercress)*

Mild sumac onions are a basic staple of many mezze ingredients, from salad to kebab. We add peppery greens, such as mustard greens or watercress, and a creamy olive oil dressing to take it to the next level!

— Peel the onions and cut into small pieces. Place them in a bowl and sprinkle them with the sumac and a little salt. Massage the mixture into the onion.

— Whisk the garlic with the lemon juice and olive oil to make a creamy dressing. Season to taste with salt.

— Just before serving, mix the sumac onions with the peppery greens and some dressing.

Armenian salad
WITH SPICY PEPPER DRESSING

— *Serves 4—6*

1 TURKISH RED PEPPER
   (*or large mild long red chilli*)
1 CARROT
2 SMALL FIRM CUCUMBERS
2 RIPE TOMATOES
1 ORGANIC LEMON
1 BUNCH PARSLEY
3 TABLESPOONS SWEET TURKISH
   RED PEPPER PASTE
   (*biber salçasi*)
60 ML (2 FL OZ/¼ CUP) LEMON
   JUICE
80 ML (2½ FL OZ/⅓ CUP) MILD-
   TASTING OLIVE OIL
TURKISH RED PEPPER FLAKES
   (*pul biber or Aleppo pepper*)
SALT

Lebanon has a rich Armenian culinary tradition and there are many Armenian restaurants with equally rich mezze menus. Every restaurant and every Armenian-Lebanese family has their own interpretation of this salad, and we do too ...

— Wash the vegetables and the lemon. Peel the lemon, then and cut everything into small cubes. Place in a salad bowl.

— Wash and dry the parsley, then finely chop and add to the bowl.

— Combine the pepper paste with the lemon juice and oil to make a dressing. Sprinkle the salad with pepper flakes and some salt. Dress and mix the salad just before serving.

Raw kibbeh
OF GOAT WITH MINT AND SEVEN SPICE

— *Serves 4—6*

300 G (10½ OZ) MINCED (GROUND)
   GOAT (*or minced lamb*)

75 G (2¾ OZ) FINE BULGHUR

2 TEASPOONS SEVEN SPICE *plus extra*

SALT FLAKES

FRESH MINT LEAVES

GOOD OLIVE OIL

RADISHES

CUCUMBER

FLATBREADS

Kibbeh has thousands of variants, most of which are baked. The base is always made with fine bulghur, which is then mixed with minced meat or potato, pumpkin (winter squash), lentils or even tomato. This is the famous raw kibbeh (similar to steak tartare), which is traditionally made from goat meat. You can, of course, also use lamb or beef. Ask your butcher to pass the mince through the grinder two or three times, because it should be as fine as possible. Goat meat can be bought from Moroccan or Turkish butchers.

— Mix the goat or lamb with the bulghur, seven spice and a good sprinkling of salt, squishing it all together with your hands to create a thick paste. Press the kibbeh onto a flat plate and use the back of a spoon to press some indents into the surface. Sprinkle with mint leaves, drizzle generously with olive oil and finish with an extra sprinkling of salt flakes and seven spice. Serve with radishes and/or cucumber, and, of course, flatbreads.

Beetroot salad
WITH SESAME AND TAHINI DRESSING

— *Serves 4–6*

5 FIRM BEETROOT (BEETS)

150 ML (5½ FL OZ) OLIVE OIL

2 GARLIC CLOVES

50 G (1¾ OZ) SESAME SEEDS

1 BUNCH SPRING ONIONS
   (SCALLIONS)

125 ML (4 FL OZ/½ CUP) TAHINI

60 ML (2 FL OZ/¼ CUP) APPLE CIDER
   VINEGAR

SALT

Red beetroots (beets) are often eaten as mezze when they are in season, and are usually served with some salt, lemon juice and parsley. We have mixed things up here and used tahini and fried sesame seeds instead.

— Scrub the beetroot and cook them whole until just tender, either by boiling them in salted water or roasting them in a hot oven. Set aside to cool.

— Heat three-quarters of the oil in a frying pan over medium–high heat and fry the garlic cloves until golden brown. Remove the garlic from the oil and add two-thirds of the sesame seeds to the same oil. Fry for a few seconds until golden, then pour the oil and seeds into a dish. Discard the garlic.

— Peel the beetroot and cut them into cubes. Clean the spring onions and finely slice. Combine the tahini with the vinegar and season with salt.

— Mix the beetroot with the spring onion just before serving. Top with a little tahini dressing and most of the sesame oil. Add the remaining olive oil, a little more salt (and vinegar if desired), to taste. Pour the remaining tahini dressing into a bowl and drizzle the rest of the sesame oil over the top. Sprinkle the salad with the remaining sesame seeds.

Lentil salad

WITH TAMARIND–GARLIC DRESSING, SHALLOT AND PARSLEY

— *Serves 2–4*

200 G (7 OZ) PUY LENTILS

2 SHALLOTS

2 TABLESPOONS RED WINE VINEGAR

SALT

2 TABLESPOONS TAMARIND PASTE

1–2 GARLIC CLOVES *grated*

150 ML (5½ FL OZ) OLIVE OIL

½ BUNCH PARSLEY *finely chopped*

This is a very simple salad, but the freshness from the tamarind works really well with the earthy lentil flavours. Legumes are indispensable on the mezzanine table.

— Boil the lentils in a large pot of salted water until cooked through.

— Peel and halve the shallots, then slice finely. Massage the vinegar into the shallot, along with a little salt.

— In a small saucepan over low heat, combine the tamarind paste, garlic and a little salt with 1–2 tablespoons hot water, and stir until the tamarind is completely dissolved. Stir in the olive oil and mix the dressing through the lentils, along with the parsley and shallot.

Moghrabieh

WITH ORANGE, SHALLOTS, SEVEN SPICE AND ALMONDS

— *Serves 4–6*

300 G (10½ OZ) MOGHRABIEH
    (*pearl/Israeli couscous*)

6 SHALLOTS

200 ML (7 FL OZ) PEANUT OIL

SALT AND PEPPER

1 TABLESPOON SEVEN SPICE
    plus extra

200 ML (7 FL OZ) ORANGE JUICE

75 G (2½ OZ) ALMONDS

2 ORANGES

125 ML (4 FL OZ/½ CUP) EXTRA-VIRGIN
    OLIVE OIL

This is not a traditional mezze salad, but we find that the combination of moghrabieh, seven spice and almonds makes for some classic Lebanese comfort food.

— Cook the moghrabieh in plenty of boiling salted water for about 15 minutes or until tender. Drain and set aside to cool until lukewarm.

— Meanwhile, peel the shallots and cut them into small pieces. Heat three-quarters of the peanut oil in a frying pan and fry the shallot until deep brown and slightly crisp. Remove the shallot from the pan and season with salt, pepper and the seven spice. Bring the orange juice to a simmer in a small saucepan and reduce to less than half. Set aside to cool.

— Heat the rest of the peanut oil and fry the almonds until golden brown and crisp. Let them cool on a plate. Grate the zest of 1 orange over the almonds, then peel and segment the oranges, separating the fruit from the pith with a sharp knife. Whisk the cooled orange juice reduction with the olive oil and season with salt and pepper. Roughly chop the almonds.

— Mix the moghrabieh with the orange juice dressing, fried shallot, almonds and orange segments. If desired, season with more pepper, salt and seven spice to taste.

Loubia bi zeit

— *Serves 4–6*

1 WHITE ONION

3 GARLIC CLOVES

125 ML (4 FL OZ/½ CUP) MILD-TASTING
 OLIVE OIL *plus extra*

5 RIPE TOMATOES

500 G (1 LB 2 OZ) FLAT BEANS

SALT AND PEPPER

Loubia bi zeit simply means chopped green beans with olive oil. We make our version with a little tomato, because we just love it when simple ingredients, such as beans, tomatoes, garlic and olive oil, meld together into something truly amazing.

— Peel the onion and garlic and finely chop. Heat the oil in a saucepan and fry the onion and garlic for a few minutes. Cut the tomatoes into chunks and add them to the onion. Wash the beans and cut them on an angle into thirds. Add to the pan with a large spoon of water and some salt and pepper to taste. Cook, covered with a lid, on medium heat for 30 minutes. Drizzle with a little more olive oil before serving.

Elephant beans
WITH ROASTED GARLIC AND CUMIN

— *Serves 4–6*

200 G (7 OZ) DRIED WHITE ELEPHANT
 BEANS OR LIMA BEANS
 soaked overnight

3 GARLIC CLOVES *sliced*

1 TABLESPOON GROUND CUMIN

2 TEASPOONS PAPRIKA

OLIVE OIL

SALT

This elephant bean salad is not traditional, but again shows how delicious beans are if you take the trouble to soak them. Simply pick up a bag of large white beans (elephant or lima) from the supermarket, soak them overnight and cook. Too easy.

— Drain the soaked beans, then boil in plenty of fresh water for 30–45 minutes, until cooked (the time will depend on how old and how dry the beans are). Drain. Fry the garlic in a dry frying pan until golden. Add the cumin, paprika and the beans. Add a large spoonful of olive oil and season well with salt. Toss it all a few times, then take the pan off the heat. Serve lukewarm or cold.

Chopped tomato salad
WITH PISTACHIOS

— *Serves 2–4*

4 RIPE ROMA OR TRUSS TOMATOES

2 RED ONIONS

175 G (6 OZ) SHELLED PISTACHIOS

1 SMALL BUNCH PARSLEY

SALT

RED WINE VINEGAR

OLIVE OIL

We just cannot get enough of salads. On the mezze table, salads should be exuberant, full of colour and flavour. And they should be easy to make! Here are two salads that do all of these things and more. Go to a Turkish shop for the very best pistachios and use the best argan oil you can find and.

— Chop the tomatoes and red onions into small cubes. Heat a dry frying pan and toast the pistachios for a few minutes until fragrant, taking care not to burn them. Allow them to cool, then chop. Finely chop the parsley. In a salad bowl, mix the tomatoes with the onion, pistachios and parsley, then dress with salt, vinegar and olive oil to taste. Serve immediately.

Potato and egg salad
WITH ARGAN OIL AND HAZELNUTS

— *Serves 2–4*

3 MEDIUM-SIZED BOILING POTATOES
cooked in boiling salted water

2 SOFT-BOILED EGGS

150 G (5½ OZ) HAZELNUTS

1 BUNCH PARSLEY

ARGAN OIL

RED WINE VINEGAR

— Chop the potatoes and eggs into small cubes. Heat a dry frying pan and toast the hazelnuts for a few minutes until fragrant, taking care not to burn them. Allow them to cool, then chop. Finely chop the parsley. In a salad bowl, mix the potato with the egg, hazelnuts and parsley, and season with salt, argan oil and a small spoon of red wine vinegar.

Tomato with toum
AND WITH SUMAC AND ARAK

— *Serves as many as you like*

BIG MEATY TOMATOES

SALT

SUMAC

ARAK OR PASTIS

6 GARLIC CLOVES

2 TABLESPOONS LEMON JUICE

150 ML (5 FL OZ) MILD-TASTING
   SUNFLOWER OIL

Toum is a beautiful Arabic garlic sauce, rather like aioli, made with garlic, lemon juice, oil and salt. For this recipe, find the most luscious tomatoes you can, ideally from a farmers' market or direct from a farmer. Or maybe you grow your own? Use a mixture of varieties for great colour and flavour. If you can't find arak, use pastis, as it's a similar style of anise liqueur.

— Cut the tomatoes into thick slices. Season with salt and sumac and sprinkle with some arak or pastis.

— To make the toum, crush the garlic and place in a small bowl with some salt and the lemon juice. Add the oil in a slow stream and whisk until emulsified. And there you have it: toum!

— Drizzle the toum over the tomatoes and serve.

Stuffed vine leaves

WITH POMEGRANATE, BARBERRIES, GRAPES AND BULGHUR

— *Serves 4–6*

ABOUT 30 VINE LEAVES
   (fresh or tinned)
2 RIPE TOMATOES
100 G (3½ OZ) FINE BULGHUR
1 BUNCH BLACK GRAPES
½ BUNCH PARSLEY
80 ML (2½ FL OZ/⅓ CUP)
   POMEGRANATE MOLASSES
80 ML (2½ FL OZ/⅓ CUP) EXTRA-
   VIRGIN OLIVE OIL
2 TABLESPOONS BARBERRIES
BLACK SALT AND PEPPER

The Ottomans never made it to Morocco, despite the reach of their conquests, so dolmades were not something I had come across. The first time I ate these spiced stuffed vine leaves, I fell in love. Since then, I've tried so many variations and twists on the classic style, and I don't think I'll ever run out of new ideas for fillings. If you have vine leaves in your garden, blanch them in boiling salted water and use them immediately, or you can even use them raw.

— If you're using fresh vine leaves, rinse them well and pat dry. If you're using tinned leaves, they can sometimes be quite salty. If so, soak them in some warm water for a few hours, changing the water every so often. Rinse and pat dry.

— Wash the tomatoes, chop them into small pieces and combine with the bulghur in a large bowl. Cut the grapes into small pieces. Wash the parsley and finely chop. Add the grapes, parsley, pomegranate molasses, olive oil and barberries to the bowl and mix well. Season with black salt and freshly ground black pepper.

— Spoon a teaspoon of filling onto each vine leaf and roll them up tight. These are delicious dipped in a sauce made of pomegranate molasses, olive oil, salt and pepper.

Freekeh salad

WITH TOMATO, POMEGRANATE, OREGANO AND ALMONDS

— *Serves 4–6*

300 G (10 OZ) CRACKED FREEKEH

125 ML (4 FL OZ/½ CUP) PEANUT OIL

100 G (3½ OZ) BLANCHED ALMONDS

4 RIPE TOMATOES

1 POMEGRANATE

1 BUNCH OREGANO

80 ML (2½ FL OZ/⅓ CUP) EXTRA-
   VIRGIN OLIVE OIL

SALT AND PEPPER

This salad, like the Moghrabieh salad on page 96, owes more to Lebanese home cooking than it does to mezze. But the smoky aromatic flavour of the freekeh, complemented by the nuttiness from the almonds and the freshness from the tomato and pomegranate, makes this one of our favourite salads — sometimes we forget that we came up with it ourselves! For a little extra bite, stir some pomegranate molasses and/or lemon juice through the freekeh.

— Boil the freekeh in plenty of salted water (the water should be as salty as the sea, as with pasta!) for 15–20 minutes. Strain and set aside to cool, then transfer to a salad bowl.

— Heat the oil in a frying pan and fry the almonds until golden brown. Let them cool, then chop them roughly.

— Cut the tomatoes in half and squeeze the seeds out over the freekeh. If you like, chop the flesh and add to the freekeh, or keep it to use for a soup or sauce. Cut the crown from the pomegranate, put both thumbs into the hole and break the pomegranate open. Break both halves into pieces. Hold the pieces above a bowl and use a wooden spoon to beat hard on the skin so that all of the seeds fall out. Remove and discard any white pith.

— Just before serving, pick the oregano leaves off the sprigs. Add three-quarters of the pomegranate seeds, the chopped almonds and three-quarters of the oregano leaves to the freekeh. Season with olive oil and some salt and pepper, and mix well. Top with the remaining pomegranate seeds and oregano.

Red lentil kibbeh
WITH FRIED ONION AND SPRING ONION

— *Serves 4–8*

400 G (14 OZ) RED LENTILS
   (or orange lentils)
2 TABLESPOONS SWEET TURKISH
   RED PEPPER PASTE
   (biber salçasi)
SALT
TURKISH RED PEPPER FLAKES
   (pul biber or Aleppo pepper)
340 G (12 OZ) EXTRA-FINE BULGHUR
4–5 ONIONS
OLIVE OIL
1 BUNCH PARSLEY
5 SPRING ONIONS (SCALLIONS)

This is a great example of a vegetarian kibbeh (along with the Pumpkin kibbeh on page 202). It comes to the mezze table via the Armenian community in Lebanon, who have enriched Lebanese mezze with their delicious dishes. This kibbeh is as simple as can be, and you can easily make it in large quantities — perfect for parties. The fried onions make the texture and flavour really great.

— Boil the lentils in plenty of water, until tender. Drain in a sieve and allow to cool. Purée the lentils with the red pepper paste, some salt and a sprinkling of red pepper flakes. Mix the bulghur into the lentils, kneading and squashing the mixture with your hands so it's very well combined.

— Peel the onions, cut them in half and then slice. Fry in a little oil until golden brown. Add to the lentils.

— Chop the parsley and the spring onions, making sure to include quite a bit of the green parts. Add to the lentils, along with a little more salt if you need, and mix well. Using your hands, shape the dough into kibbeh shapes, as you can see in the picture. Eat straight away, or save them for your lunch tomorrow!

Warm mezze

Warm mezze is sometimes so filling and delicious that we don't even get to the main course! It's certainly difficult to go further than our huge mezze menu — there are so many tasty dishes to choose from or to think about, with classics and new favourites.

There's so much to choose from our kibbeh varieties alone. Kibbeh has many interpretations, from Lebanon to Syria and Turkey to Iraq. The shape varies from ovals and large flat discs to round balls or large square plate kibbeh. Bulghur is always the base, kneaded with meat or, vegetarian-style with potato, pumpkin (winter squash) or lentils.

The *batata harra*, literally 'hot potatoes', are a must on your warm mezze table. They are a mouth-watering combination of fried potato, lemon, pepper and coriander (cilantro) ...

ليمون

Fatayer

— *Makes about 20*

2 TEASPOONS DRIED YEAST

EXTRA-VIRGIN OLIVE OIL

60 G (2 OZ/¼ CUP) TURKISH YOGHURT

SALT

300 G (10½ OZ) WHOLEGRAIN SPELT
FLOUR *plus extra*

1 RED ONION

½ HOT GREEN CHILLI

100 G (3½ OZ) WILD SPINACH

3 TABLESPOONS SUMAC

2 TABLESPOONS POMEGRANATE
MOLASSES

1 TEASPOON GROUND CINNAMON

BEATEN EGG *(optional)*

MELTED BUTTER *(optional)*

Fatayer can be time-consuming to make, but they're still quite simple to prepare. We always make a mountain of these at a time and store them baked or unbaked in the freezer, ready for the next mezze. The filling here is slightly sour, which makes these a perfect snack with a few drinks.

— Stir a spoon of lukewarm water through the yeast and set aside until it looks foamy. In a mixing bowl, combine 50 ml (1¾ fl oz) olive oil with the yoghurt and a large pinch of salt. Stir in the spelt flour, the yeast mixture and enough warm water to bring it together into a cohesive dough. Cover the bowl with plastic wrap and set aside in a warm, draught-free place for about 2 hours.

— Peel the onion, cut it in half and then finely slice. Place the onion in a sieve and massage in some salt. Finely chop the chilli and add to the onion. Place the sieve over a bowl to drain, then set aside for a while to allow the salt to draw out some of the moisture from the onions. Chop the spinach, combine it with a little salt, then squeeze the spinach well to remove some of the moisture. Mix the spinach and half the sumac with the onion and set aside to keep draining for a little longer. Squeeze as much liquid out of the mixture as you can, then transfer to a mixing bowl and add the remaining sumac, the pomegranate molasses, cinnamon and a slug of olive oil.

— On a well-floured work surface, roll the dough out until very thin. Cut into circles about 10 cm (4 in) in diameter. Place some filling in the middle of each circle, fold the sides up to make a pyramid shape and press the pastry together to seal the edges.

— Preheat the oven to 200°C (400°F) and line a baking tray with baking paper. Brush the fatayer with some olive oil or beaten egg. Bake the fatayer in the oven on the prepared tray for about 15 minutes until golden brown and cooked. Lightly drizzle with olive oil or melted butter, if desired, and serve warm.

Here is another member of the extended kibbeh family. This is one of the more laborious kinds: first you make kibbeh 'dough' (minced/ground lamb or beef mixed with bulghur) into balls or cup shapes, and then you stuff them with a filling before they are fried or baked. But they are well worth the effort, we promise! The more you practise making them, the better you'll get. What's more, you can make them in large batches and freeze them, and then all you need to do is bake or fry them as needed. Either way, your efforts will always be rewarded, because this world is full of people who love kibbeh!

If you are going to make kibbeh, ask your butcher to pass the lamb mince two or three times through the grinder as you want a fine texture. We used goat mince for the photo, so the colour is slightly darker.

Baked kibbeh balls

— *Serves 4–8*

2 LARGE ONIONS

OLIVE OIL

3 TABLESPOONS PINE NUTS

400 G (14 OZ) MINCED (GROUND)
    LAMB

1 TEASPOON GROUND
    CINNAMON

1 TEASPOON SUMAC

1 TABLESPOON POMEGRANATE
    MOLASSES

1 TABLESPOON SEVEN SPICE

125 G (4½ OZ) FINE BULGHUR

SALT

OIL *for frying*

— To make the filling, finely chop one of the onions and fry it in a little olive oil over low heat for 10 minutes. Add the pine nuts and cook for a further 5 minutes, then add 150 g (5½ oz) of the mince, along with the cinnamon, sumac, pomegranate molasses and 2 teaspoons of the seven spice. Cook for a further 5 minutes, then remove from the heat.

— Grate the remaining onion and place in a food processor, along with the rest of the mince and seven spice, the bulghur, a small spoon of water and a little salt. Process until smooth. Knead the dough a little – it should be firm but not dry.

— Using damp hands, divide the dough into balls about 2–3 cm (¾–1¼ in) in diameter and make a dent in each using your thumb. Place one ball in the palm of your hand and widen the dent with your thumb. Gently turn your thumb around until the dough becomes thinner and the ball looks like an oval cup. This may seem complicated, but you'll get the hang of it after you've made a few!

— Put 2 teaspoons of filling into each 'cup' and press the dough closed around the filling, making sure it's smooth and well sealed, and resembles the shape shown in the photo. Repeat with the remaining dough balls and filling. Deep-fry the kibbeh balls or bake them in a preheated 200°C (400°F) oven until golden brown.

Roasted octopus and charred eggplant

WITH TAHINI AND ORANGE

— *Serves 4—6*

1 BUNCH PARSLEY

1 ORANGE

4 GARLIC CLOVES

BLACK PEPPERCORNS

COARSE SEA SALT

1 OCTOPUS *cleaned*

200 ML (7 FL OZ) ORANGE JUICE

2 FIRM EGGPLANTS (AUBERGINES)

2 TABLESPOONS TAHINI

FRESHLY GROUND BLACK PEPPER

80 ML (2½ FL OZ/⅓ CUP) OLIVE OIL

Inspired by the modern Middle Eastern style of The Palomar in London, this is a dish we make time and time again. The charred eggplant (aubergine) gives the octopus a wonderful kick, while the citrus and nutty tahini finish makes this a new dish that tastes very familiar.

— Pick the leaves from the parsley and set aside. Keeps the stalks and tie them in a bundle with butcher's twine. Peel half the zest of the orange into strips and finely grate the remainder of the zest. Peel the garlic cloves and place two of them in a large saucepan with 1.5 litres (1½ qts) water, the parsley stalks, strips of orange zest, some peppercorns and a big pinch of salt. Bring to the boil, then reduce the heat to its lowest setting and carefully place the octopus into the water. Cook for about 1 hour, then turn off the heat and leave to cool completely. Drain and pat the octopus dry.

— Juice the orange into a small saucepan and simmer over medium heat until reduced by more than half. Set aside to cool.

— Heat a barbecue grill to high. Cook the eggplants until the outside is charred and the flesh is soft. Making sure the grill is still very hot, char the octopus quickly on all sides.

— Peel the eggplants and chop the flesh. Season the tahini with some salt and pepper. Finely chop the parsley leaves and the remaining garlic. Chop the octopus into pieces and mix with the garlic, parsley and grated orange zest.

— Spread the eggplant onto a nice serving dish. Top with the tahini and octopus. Drizzle with the reduced orange juice and the olive oil.

Roasted cauliflower

WITH TAHINI, NUTS AND MINT

— *Serves 12–16*

2 HEADS CAULIFLOWERS
  (*with green leaves attached*)

SALT

50 G (1¾ OZ) ROASTED HAZELNUTS

50 G (1¾ OZ) SUNFLOWER SEEDS

3 TABLESPOONS ROASTED SESAME
  SEEDS

1 GARLIC CLOVE

200 ML (7 FL OZ) TAHINI

1 LEMON

1 TABLESPOON DRIED MINT

FRESHLY GROUND BLACK PEPPER

EXTRA-VIRGIN OLIVE OIL

This is a vegetable dish that is a more-than-worthy meat substitute for your mezze table. Of course, it's not just a meat substitute: you'll eat so much of this dish that you forget about meat altogether.

— Preheat the oven to 200°C (400°F) or a barbecue grill to high. Wash the cauliflowers and sprinkle them generously with salt. Place them in the middle of the oven, or in the barbecue with the lid closed and roast for 30–45 minutes (depending on the size of the cauliflowers), until tender and golden.

— Meanwhile, chop the hazelnuts and sunflower seeds and combine them with the sesame seeds. Zest the lemon and squeeze the juice into a bowl. Peel the garlic clove and chop finely. Mix the tahini with the lemon juice and a spoon of water, then stir in the nuts and seeds, lemon zest, garlic, dried mint, and salt and pepper to taste.

— Serve the cauliflowers whole drizzled with the topping and a little olive oil. Everyone will be impressed!

Fried fish
WITH SUMAC AND LEMON LABNE AND CRISPY TARRAGON

— *Serves 4—6*

COARSE SEA SALT

500 G (1 LB 2 OZ/2 CUPS) YOGHURT

8–12 SMALL CLEANED FISH
   (such as sardines or mackerel)

OIL *for frying*

2 LEMONS

1 TABLESPOON SUMAC

1 SMALL BUNCH TARRAGON

FLATBREADS *to serve*

The mixture of labne, sumac and lemon combine to make this a beautifully complex dish. First, you taste the aromatic lemon, then the creamy dairy, and you finish with the fresh floral flavour of sumac. This all makes for a lovely complement to the fried fish.

— Stir 2 teaspoons of salt through the yoghurt. Place a clean square of muslin (cheesecloth) on your work surface and spoon the yoghurt on top. Tie up the corners to create a bag, then transfer to a colander set over a bowl or saucepan. Place in the fridge and leave for at least 4 hours (for soft labne) or overnight (for firm labne), making sure the yoghurt doesn't touch the drained whey.

— Wash the fish, then pat dry with paper towel and sprinkle with some salt. Heat the oil in a frying pan and fry the fish, turning 2–3 times, until golden brown, crisp and cooked through. Drain on paper towel. Fry the sprigs of tarragon for a few seconds, until crisp, and drain on paper towel as well.

— Squeeze the juice of one of the lemons over the labne. Add the sumac and stir to combine. Spread the labne onto plates and top with the fried fish. Scatter with the crispy tarragon and serve alongside the flatbreads. Cut the remaining lemon into pieces for squeezing over the fish.

Round goat kibbeh
WITH GOAT'S LABNE AND FRIED ONIONS

— *Serves 4–6*

SALT

150 G (5½ OZ) THICK GOAT'S YOGHURT

4 ONIONS

OLIVE OIL

30 G (1 OZ) PINE NUTS

300 G (10½ OZ) MINCED (GROUND)
    GOAT *(ground very fine)*

150 G (5½ OZ) FINE BULGHUR

2 TABLESPOONS SEVEN SPICE

1 TEASPOON CINNAMON

POMEGRANATE MOLASSES *(optional)*

This round kibbeh is not classic, but it looks similar to kibbeh sajia from Aleppo. In the north of Lebanon, they often use firm labne as a filling in the kibbeh. The combination of the goat mince (this is our last rave, by the way, but goat is so delicious!) with the goat's labne is pretty sublime.

— Stir 2 teaspoons of salt through the yoghurt. Place a clean square of muslin (cheesecloth) on your work surface and spoon the yoghurt on top. Tie up the corners to create a bag, then transfer to a colander set over a bowl or saucepan. Place in the fridge and eave to drain overnight, making sure the yoghurt doesn't touch the drained whey.

— Cut the onions in half and then slice. Fry them in olive oil over low heat, stirring often, for about 30 minutes, until golden brown. Add the pine nuts and fry until golden.

— Knead the goat mince, bulghur, a little salt, the seven spice and cinnamon together to form a 'dough'.

— Preheat the oven to 200°C (400°F). Line a baking tray with baking paper. Divide the dough in half, and then divide one of the halves into balls 5–6 cm (2–2¼ in) in diameter. Squash them into nice flat rounds by placing a ball on a square of baking paper, covering it with another square of baking paper and using a flat-bottomed tray to press down. Transfer the rounds to the lined baking tray, then spoon some of the onion mixture, a little labne and, if you like, a drizzle of pomegranate molasses in the middle. Make the rounds again with the other half of the dough and use these to cover the filled ones on the tray. Press along the edges to seal each kibbeh well. Brush the tops with some oil and bake in the oven for 15–20 minutes, until golden brown and cooked.

Rakakat
WITH HALOUMI, FETA AND PARSLEY

— *Makes 10–15*

SUNFLOWER OIL

375 G (13 OZ) FILO PASTRY

1 SMALL BUNCH PARSLEY
   separated into sprigs

250 G (9 OZ) HALOUMI *sliced into*
   thin strips

200 G (7 OZ) FETA *crumbled*

OIL *for frying*

A classic on any warm mezze menu and rightly so, with their crispy dough and melting cheese. We see customers go crazy for these bad boys, especially when they're fresh and golden, straight from the pan. There are also versions with yufka dough (the best known being the Turkish börek), but our favourite is this version, made with crisp filo pastry and a combination of salty haloumi and feta (instead of feta on its own) works very well. For this recipe, seek out a good Mediterranean grocer and find youself a nice big roll of top-quality filo from the fridge.

— Make sure you have a clean damp tea towel and a small bowl of sunflower oil ready to go.

— Remove the filo from the packet, and cover with the tea towel. Take one sheet of filo and cut it vertically into two pieces. Put one piece back under the tea towel.

— Lay the other piece on your work surface with the short end facing you. Place a few sprigs of parsley near the end closest to you and fold the edge of the filo over the parsley. Rub the folded pastry with a little sunflower oil. Next, make a line of haloumi and crumbled feta along the end closest to you, then fold in the long edges about 1.5 cm (½ in), and roll the whole thing up into a neat cigar shape. Seal the end with a little sunflower oil. Repeat with the remaining filling and pastry, working fast so that the pastry doesn't dry out.

— Heat the oil to 180°C (350°F) or until a cube of bread dropped into the oil turns golden brown in 30 seconds. Fry the cigars, in batches, until golden brown. Drain on paper towel and eat immediately.

Haloumi from the oven
WITH BREAD, DATES AND ZA'ATAR

— *Serves 4–6*

225 G (8 OZ) HALOUMI

2 FLATBREADS

EXTRA-VIRGIN OLIVE OIL

20 PITTED DATES

4 TABLESPOONS ZA'ATAR

This dish is perfect to eat with your hands, and the super-sweet dates are fantastic with the salt of the cheese and the spicy za'atar. This dish really has everything: sweet, salty, spicy, creamy, nutty, crispy, soft. A real umami bomb!

— Preheat the oven to 200°C (400°F). Line a baking tray with baking paper. Cut the haloumi into slices.

— Tear the flatbreads into pieces and scatter them, along with the haloumi, onto the prepared tray. Drizzle with olive oil and mix to coat. Add the dates and sprinkle generously with the za'atar. Place in the middle of the oven and cook for about 15 minutes, until the bread and cheese are golden brown and the dates are nicely caramelised.

— Serve warm, but be careful: the dates will stay very hot for a long time!

Sucuk and chicken liver

WITH SUMAC AND POMEGRANATE MOLASSES

— *Serves 4–6*

300 G (10½ OZ) SUCUK SAUSAGES

3 GARLIC CLOVES

60 ML (2 FL OZ/¼ CUP) MILD-TASTING
  OLIVE OIL

3 TABLESPOONS SUMAC

300 G (10½ OZ) CHICKEN LIVERS

SALT AND PEPPER

80 ML (2½ FL OZ/⅓ CUP)
  POMEGRANATE MOLASSES

A mezze classic from Armenian, Lebanese and Turkish cuisines. We understand why this dish has been hit for decades ... it's so simple!

— Cut the sucuk into slices. Peel and slice the garlic. Heat the oil in a frying pan and fry the sucuk on both sides until golden brown and cooked. Tip the sucuk out of the pan and sprinkle with half of the sumac.

— Return the pan to the stovetop and fry the garlic and chicken livers for a few minutes, until golden brown and cooked. Sprinkle with some salt and pepper and the remaining sumac and toss to combine.

— Slide the chicken livers to one side of the pan, and return the sucuk to the other side. Drizzle everything with the pomegranate molasses and warm briefly. Serve hot.

Batata harra

WITH CORIANDER, LEMON AND PUL BIBER

— *Serves 4—6*

1 KG (2 LB 3 OZ) BABY POTATOES

4 GARLIC CLOVES

1 BUNCH CORIANDER (CILANTRO)

1 LEMON

SALT AND PEPPER

125 ML (4 FL OZ/½ CUP) OLIVE OIL

TURKISH RED PEPPER FLAKES

  (*pul biber or Aleppo pepper*)

Lebanese preparations of potato are divine, whether it's potato kibbeh or chopped potato chips. But *batata harra*, or 'hot potato', is perhaps the most indulgent: crispy potato on the outside, creamy soft flesh inside, and flavoured with fresh lemon, spicy garlic, coriander (cilantro) and hot red pepper flakes. What more could a potato lover wish for?

— Preheat the oven to 240°C (450°F). Line a baking tray with baking paper.

— Wash the potatoes and cut them into small cubes. Peel and finely chop the garlic. Wash and dry the coriander and finely chop the leaves and sprigs. Grate the zest of the lemon and squeeze out the juice.

— Spread the potato on the prepared tray. Sprinkle over two-thirds of the garlic, and half of the coriander, lemon zest and lemon juice. Season with salt and pepper, then pour over the oil. Toss to combine, then bake for about 30 minutes, or until crisp and golden brown.

— Toss the cooked potato with the remaining garlic, coriander, lemon zest and juice, and season with red pepper flakes and a little more salt if you need. Serve the batata harra hot, lukewarm or cold.

Armenian stuffed carrots

IN TAMARIND, POMEGRANATE AND COFFEE SAUCE

— *Serves 4–6*

3 VERY LARGE CARROTS

300 G (10½ OZ) MINCED (GROUND)
    LAMB

60 G (2 OZ) SHORT-GRAIN RICE

1 GARLIC CLOVE

3 CLOVES

2 TEASPOONS SEVEN SPICE

1 TABLESPOON GROUND CINNAMON

SALT AND PEPPER

3 TABLESPOONS TAMARIND PASTE

60 ML (2 FL OZ/¼ CUP) ESPRESSO

100 ML (3½ FL OZ) POMEGRANATE
    MOLASSES

FLAT-LEAF PARSLEY OR CORIANDER
    (CILANTRO) *finely chopped*

We ate these stuffed carrots in Beirut and were completely overwhelmed. The combination of spicy cloves and sweet–sour pomegranate molasses with the carrot is really delicious.

— Clean the carrots and cut them into 5 cm (2 in) lengths. Core each piece of carrot (we use an apple corer). Boil the carrots until they are just tender.

— Mix the lamb with the rice. Peel the garlic and, using a mortar and pestle, crush well with the cloves, then add to the mince and rice mixture along with the seven spice, cinnamon and some salt and pepper to season. Fill the carrot pieces with the meat mixture, then place the stuffed carrots upright in a pan with a lid.

— In a small bowl, combine the tamarind paste, espresso, pomegranate molasses, a spoonful of water and some salt and pepper, then add to the pan. Place over low–medium heat and cook with the lid partially off for about 25 minutes, adding some extra water if it boils dry, until the rice is tender.

— Serve warm, sprinkled with the parsley or coriander.

Turmeric lentil soup
WITH LEMON YOGHURT

— *Serves 4–6*

3 ONIONS

3 GARLIC CLOVES

80 ML (2½ FL OZ/⅓ CUP) MILD-
   TASTING OLIVE OIL

200 G (7 OZ) RED LENTILS

4 TABLESPOONS GROUND TURMERIC

2 TABLESPOONS SWEET RAS EL
   HANOUT *plus extra to serve*

SALT AND PEPPER

200 G (7 OZ) TURKISH YOGHURT

½ LEMON

Soup is not very traditional for mezze but this Turkish-style dish is so beautiful for autumn and winter. This golden-yellow soup is very quick to make, but because of the turmeric and ras el hanout, and the rich base of fried onion and garlic, it tastes like something that's been simmering away for hours. How fantastic is that?

— Peel and finely chop the onions and garlic. Set aside about ½ teaspoon of the garlic. Heat the oil in a saucepan over low–medium heat and fry the onion and garlic for about 10 minutes. Add the lentils, turmeric and ras el hanout and stir until fragrant. Add 150 ml (5 fl oz) water and season with salt and pepper. Cook the lentils for about 20 minutes, adding more water if necessary, until soft and broken down. If you like, purée the soup at the end of cooking with a hand-held blender.

— Stir the reserved chopped garlic through the yoghurt and grate the zest of the lemon over the top. Add a little salt to taste and, if you like, some lemon juice.

— Ladle the hot soup into warm bowls and top with a spoonful of the lemony yoghurt and a sprinkling of ras el hanout. Serve the rest of the yoghurt in a small bowl on the table.

Freekeh soup

WITH SEVEN SPICE, ONION AND PUMPKIN

— *Serves 4–6*

1 SMALL PUMPKIN (WINTER SQUASH)

SALT

MILD-TASTING OLIVE OIL

5 ONIONS *sliced*

1 TABLESPOON SEVEN SPICE

250 G (9 OZ) CRACKED FREEKEH

Sometimes we are not sure about a recipe and end up being really surprised by the results. We certainly were in this case! This recipe is just so simple, we never expected it to taste so good. This soup has — wait for it — no more than six ingredients.

— Preheat the oven to 200°C (400°F). Halve the pumpkin and scoop out the seeds with a spoon (but do not peel). Sprinkle with salt and olive oil, then roast the pumpkin for about 20 minutes. Reduce the oven temperature to 180°C (350°F) and keep roasting the pumpkin until it is completely soft.

— Heat a large spoon of olive oil over low–medium heat and fry the onion, stirring very often, for 30 minutes, until golden brown. Set aside about one-third of the fried onion, leaving the rest in the pan

— Add the seven spice, freekeh and 1.5 litres (1½ qts) water to the pan. Cook the freekeh in the onion broth for about 15 minutes and season well with salt. Remove the pumpkin from the oven. Scoop the flesh out with a spoon and add it to the soup.

— Serve the soup in small bowls, topped with the reserved onion. The soup is also delicious with some yoghurt mixed with sumac.

Baharat meatballs

IN SWEET AND SOUR CHERRY SAUCE WITH SUMAC YOGHURT

— *Serves 4–6*

2 ONIONS

3 GARLIC CLOVES

500 G (1 LB 2 OZ) MINCED (GROUND) LAMB

3 TABLESPOONS MIDDLE EASTERN BAHARAT

SALT AND PEPPER

2 TABLESPOONS MILD-TASTING OLIVE OIL

2 × 360 G (12½ OZ) JARS SOUR CHERRY JAM

LEMON JUICE (*optional*)

200 G (7 OZ) TURKISH YOGHURT

3 TABLESPOONS SUMAC

This is also another famous Lebanese–Armenian mezze classic. We make this with the amazing sour cherry jam you find in Turkish grocers. Let the meatballs simmer on low heat in the sauce so that they don't get too dry.

— Peel the onions and garlic and grate them finely. Mix the lamb with the onion and garlic, 2 tablespoons of the baharat, and season with salt and pepper. Shape into golf ball–sized balls using damp hands.

— Heat the oil in a saucepan over medium heat and add the rest of the baharat and the sour cherry jam. Gently bring to the boil. Add salt and pepper to taste and some lemon juice, if desired. Place the meatballs into the sauce and simmer, covered, over low heat for about 20 minutes, or until the meatballs are cooked through. If the sauce becomes too thick, add a spoonful of hot water.

— In a small bowl, mix the yoghurt with the sumac. Serve the baharat meatballs in the sauce, with the sumac yoghurt alongside.

Fried eggplant
WITH WALNUT TARATOR

— *Serves 2–4*

2 EGGPLANTS (AUBERGINES)

CORNFLOUR (CORN STARCH)

OIL *for frying*

SALT

200 G (7 OZ) WALNUTS

1 GARLIC CLOVE

1 SMALL BUNCH PARSLEY
   finely chopped

60 ML (2 FL OZ/¼ CUP) MILK

LEMON JUICE

OLIVE OIL

FLATBREADS *to serve*

Dusting the eggplant (aubergine) in cornflour (corn starch) before frying gives it an amazing crisp texture. Tarator is a sauce with many faces: in Lebanon it is usually made with tahini, but this version, made with walnuts, is what you'll find in Turkey and Eastern Europe. Personally, we find all types of tarator delicious. This one goes particularly well with the creamy, nutty flavour of the fried eggplant.

— Cut the eggplants into pieces and dredge them in the cornflour, shaking off any excess. Heat the oil to 180°C (350°F), or until a cube of bread dropped into the oil turns golden brown in 30 seconds. Fry the eggplant until golden brown, then let the pieces drain on paper towel and sprinkle with some salt.

— Roast the walnuts in a dry frying pan and allow to cool. Using a stick blender, purée the walnuts with the garlic, half the parsley and the milk. Season to taste with lemon juice and salt, and finish off with a generous slug of olive oil.

— Place the eggplant in a bowl, spoon the tarator over the top and sprinkle with the remaining parsley. Serve with flatbreads.

Mujardara

WITH A SALAD OF FRESH OREGANO, MINT, SPRING ONION AND RADISH

— *Serves 4–6*

4 ONIONS

MILD-TASTING OLIVE OIL

150 G (5½ OZ) RICE

150 G (5½ OZ) BROWN LENTILS

(you can use puy lentils or ordinary
lentils; check the packaging and
follow the instructions if they need
to be pre-cooked or soaked)

OREGANO AND MINT SPRIGS

leaves picked and finely chopped

THICK YOGHURT

2 SPRING ONIONS (SCALLIONS)

halved lengthways

BUNCH OF RADISHES

Another classic we can't do without. This is great Lebanese comfort food, but served in small portions it makes a perfect addition to the mezze table. A simple dish in which, once again, the onion (you've probably never fried so many onions, ha!) plays an integral role.

— Peel the onions, cut them in half and then slice. Gently fry them in a spoonful of olive oil for about 30 minutes, stirring often, until deep golden brown. Set aside most of the fried onion, but keep about one large spoonful in the pan. Add the rice and lentils to the pan, along with 400 ml (13½ fl oz) salted water. Bring to a simmer and cook for about 20 minutes, adding a little extra water if the mixture dries out.

— Transfer to a dish and top with the reserved fried onions. Sprinkle with the herbs and serve with a bowl of yoghurt drizzled with olive oil and the spring onion and radishes alongside.

Fried eggs
WITH LABNE, SUMAC AND NIGELLA SEEDS

— *Serves 2–4*

SALT

THICK GREEK OR TURKISH
  YOGHURT

OLIVE OIL

4 EGGS

SUMAC

NIGELLA SEEDS

FLATBREADS

If you have small earthenware dishes like the ones shown in the picture, do use them as they make all the difference to this recipe. You can usually find them for sale in Moroccan or Spanish grocers. This recipe is inspired by the incredible breakfast we ate in Beit Douma in Lebanon, freshly made by our friend Kamal.

— Stir a little salt through the yoghurt to season. Place a square of clean muslin (cheesecloth) on a work surface and spoon the yoghurt on top. Tie up the corners to create a bag, then transfer to a colander set over a bowl or saucepan to drain. Transfer to the fridge and leave for 1 hour to make a soft labne, making sure the yoghurt doesn't touch the drained whey.

— Heat a generous amount of oil in one large or two small flameproof earthernware dishes over high heat and break in the eggs. Fry the eggs for a few minutes before removing from the heat. Top with a dollop of labne and sprinkle with salt, sumac and nigella seeds. Eat with fresh flatbreads.

Baked sweet potato
WITH ARGAN OIL AND DUKKAH

Dukkah — the Egyptian mixture of nuts and spices — is everywhere nowadays. It's no wonder, because it's so versatile — it's great on eggs, avocado toast and roasted vegetables. This combination of spicy, nutty dukkah and argan oil is like a flavour explosion.

— Preheat the oven to 200°C (400°F). Wrap the potatoes in foil and bake in the oven for 45–60 minutes (depending on their size), until completely soft. Cut them open with a sharp knife and squeeze them a little. Sprinkle generously with dukkah and coarse salt, and drizzle with argan oil.

— *Serves 2–4*

4 MEDIUM-SIZED ORANGE
  SWEET POTATOES
4–6 TABLESPOONS DUKKAH
  (see the recipe opposite or use store-bought dukkah)
COARSE SALT
ARGAN OIL

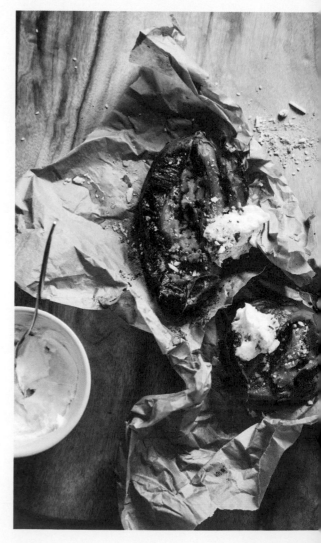

Dukkah

— *Makes 600 g (1 lb 5 oz)*

200 G (7 OZ) ROASTED DRIED
    CHICKPEAS (GARBANZO BEANS)
    (available from Turkish or
    Moroccan grocers)

300 G (10½ OZ) ROASTED ALMONDS

100 G (3½ OZ) UNTOASTED SESAME
    SEEDS

5 TABLESPOONS CORIANDER SEEDS

2 TABLESPOONS CUMIN SEEDS

3 TABLESPOONS ANISEEDS

2 TABLESPOONS FENNEL SEEDS

2 TABLESPOONS DRIED OREGANO

3 TABLESPOONS TOASTED SESAME
    SEEDS

Dukkah is great to have in your pantry. Our favourite way to serve it is in a dish sprinkled with rose petals and orange zest, and with a bowl of extra-virgin olive oil and good Arabic flatbread on the side. Dip the bread first into the olive oil and then into the dukkah. Serve with tomato, cucumber, mint and olives for a full breakfast, lunch or snack!

— Preheat the oven to 180°C (350°F). Spread all of the ingredients (except for the toasted sesame seeds) onto a baking tray or dish and bake for about 8 minutes, until fragrant. Give everything a bit of a stir a few times while baking. Tip into a spice grinder and buzz to a medium-fine grind. Stir the toasted sesame seeds through and store in an airtight container.

Fried prawns

WITH ARAK, GARLIC AND PEPPER

— *Serves 2–4*

4–8 LARGE RAW PRAWNS (SHRIMP)
  (*look for dark red deep-sea prawns*)

MILD-TASTING OLIVE OIL

4 LARGE GARLIC CLOVES
  finely chopped

ARAK, RAKI, OUZO OR PASTIS

SALT

TURKISH RED PEPPER FLAKES
  (*pul biber or Aleppo pepper*)

This is so simple and so tasty. The anise flavour from the alcohol is amazing with the prawns (shrimp) — a divine bite from the sea. This dish actually has Greek influences, so ouzo is a great option instead of arak.

— Cut the prawns in half lengthways. Heat a little olive oil in a frying pan over high heat, then add the prawns and the garlic. Cook for 2–3 minutes, then add a spoonful of arak, raki, ouzo or pastis. Cook briefly until the smell of alcohol disappears and the prawns are cooked through. Season with salt and red pepper flakes and serve immediately.

als hij. Ook andere sterre
dio. Zijn geheim heeft hij
Je moet me n
verwarren
roducer
bepaal
op de
kwa
Rudy Van Gelder in 2006 over zijn
Rudy Van Gelder.
sack liet opnemen.
laten die Rudy Van Gel

Artichokes in fresh tomato sauce

WITH TURMERIC AND PRESERVED LEMON

— *Serves 2–4*

4 FRESH ARTICHOKES *(if unavailable, use frozen artichoke hearts)*

LEMON JUICE

1 ONION

1 GARLIC CLOVE

4 RIPE TRUSS TOMATOES

½ PRESERVED LEMON

OLIVE OIL

1 TEASPOON GROUND TURMERIC

SALT AND PEPPER

This dish is divine in the summer when artichokes are in season. Preserved lemon is one of our favourite Moroccan ingredients and the fresh, sour, aromatic flavour is the perfect match with the nutty artichoke. This dish is a new classic!

— To clean the artichokes, first remove most of the outer petals with your hands. Using a shape knife, peel the artichokes as you would an apple, until you reach the heart. Cut the hearts, into quarters and place in some water mixed with lemon juice.

— Finely chop the onion, garlic, tomatoes and preserved lemon. Heat a large spoon of olive oil in a frying pan with a lid over low heat and add the onion and garlic. Cook, stirring often, for about 10 minutes. Add the tomato, turmeric, lemon and artichoke. Let the artichoke gently simmer over low heat with the lid on the pan, until it is cooked through. Sprinkle with salt and pepper and drizzle with another spoonful of olive oil, then serve.

The first time we ate musakahn —
a dish of baked chicken and bread
— was in Palestine, where it is
eaten to celebrate the first harvest
of the new olive oil. It's almost
impossible to stop eating this dish
once you have started.

We've made a mini version of
the tradional dish here, as a real
showpiece for the mezze table.
The combination of bread, olive
oil, sumac, onion and chicken
is incomparable. And a mini
musakhan is better for you, too —
we promise! Use the most
delicious olive oil you can find,
preferably a fresh one.

Mini-musakhan
WITH LAYERS OF BREAD, ONION, ALMONDS AND SUMAC

— *Serves 2—4*

1 TEASPOON DRIED YEAST

300 G (10½ OZ) FLOUR

1 TEASPOON SALT

4 TABLESPOONS SUMAC

4 LARGE GARLIC CLOVES

4 ORGANIC SKIN-ON BONELESS
   CHICKEN THIGHS

4 ONIONS

OLIVE OIL

100 G (3½ OZ) BLANCHED
   ALMONDS *coarsely chopped*

THICK YOGHURT

SMALL HANDFUL PARSLEY LEAVES

EXTRA-VIRGIN OLIVE OIL
   of the best quality, to serve

— Mix the yeast with a little lukewarm water and set aside until it's foamy. Mix the yeast water with the flour, salt and 1 tablespoon of the sumac, and as much lukewarm water as needed to create a cohesive, but not wet, dough. Knead the dough for 10 minutes and place it in a covered bowl in a warm spot to rise.

— Preheat the oven to 200°C (400°F). Grate the garlic, combine with 2 tablespoons of sumac and rub onto the chicken. Place in a baking dish and set aside.

— Cut the onions in half and slice. Heat a large spoon of olive oil in a frying pan and fry the onion with the remaining tablespoon of sumac and some salt. Cook for 15 minutes over low heat. Toast the almonds until golden brown and add them to the onion.

— Drizzle the chicken with a large spoon of olive oil. Bake for 10 minutes, then reduce the temperature to 180°C (350°F) and cook for about 30 minutes, until cooked through and golden brown. Set aside to rest, covered with foil.

— Knead the bread dough for a few minutes and divide into at least eight equal-sized pieces. Roll out into rounds. Heat a dry griddle or cast-iron frying pan and cook the flatbreads for a few seconds on each side.

— Slice the chicken. Purée some yoghurt and the parsley with a little salt. Place a piece of flatbread on a plate and top with some chicken and onion. Drizzle with the extra-virgin olive oil (if you want to feel like a real Palestinian, use a lot of oil, just like we do) and add another flatbread. Top again with chicken, onion and olive oil (we do two layers per serve), then repeat with the remaining ingredients. Serve with some parsley yoghurt. Blissful.

Balila

WITH LEMON AND CUMIN

— *Serves 2–4 (or more)*

1 QUANTITY HUMMUS *(page 52)*

SALT

80 G (2¾ OZ/½ CUP) COOKED
   CHICKPEAS (GARBANZO BEANS)

2 GARLIC CLOVES

25 G (¾ OZ) PINE NUTS

OLIVE OIL

LEMON JUICE

GROUND CUMIN

Balila and fatteh (see opposite) are actually breakfast dishes, which you eat as a large portion (after which you'll be very full until lunchtime). But we always like to serve them on the mezze table. They are hot and soft and crisp at the same time, with the perfect balance of creamy and tart flavours. It's impossible to miss these dishes if you ever go to the Middle East; you'll find them on every table.

— Heat the hummus in a saucepan over low heat. Add a spoon of water to make it smooth and season with a little salt. In another saucepan, heat the chickpeas in enough water to cover. Finely chop the garlic and fry with the pine nuts in a large spoonful of olive oil, until golden brown. Drain the chickpeas.

— Place the warm hummus in a bowl and toss the chickpeas with the pine nuts and garlic, as well as some olive oil, lemon juice and ground cumin to taste. Alternatively, you can blend the hummus with the olive oil, lemon juice and ground cumin. Top with the fried garlic and pine nuts.

Fatteh
WITH EGGPLANT

— *Serves 2–4*

1–2 EGGPLANTS (AUBERGINES)

OIL *for deep-frying*

2 FLATBREADS

OLIVE OIL

SALT

1 GARLIC CLOVE

NATURAL YOGHURT

100 G (3½ OZ) COOKED CHICKPEAS
    (GARBANZO BEANS)

2 TABLESPOONS BUTTER

SMALL HANDFUL PINE NUTS

Fatteh has many variants, but it's always a mix of chickpeas with yoghurt, garlic, pine nuts, hot butter and crispy bread (like you'd find in fattoush). Sometimes it's topped with fried eggplant (aubergine) and stewed lamb. This is a hearty dish and a good serve of fatteh will get you through the day. But because it's such a nice dish, we love to make a small version for the mezze table. This version has no meat.

— Cut the eggplants into medium-sized cubes. Heat the oil to 180°C (350°F) or until a cube of bread dropped into the oil turns golden brown in 30 seconds. Fry the eggplant until golden brown and leave to drain on paper towel.

— Heat a grill (broiler) to medium–high. Tear the flatbread into pieces, then toss on a baking tray with some olive oil and salt. Grill (broil) until golden brown. Grate the garlic and stir into a few spoonfuls of yoghurt seasoned with salt. Divide the chickpeas and fried eggplant among serving bowls. Spoon the garlic yoghurt over the top and cover with the crispy bread.

— Heat the butter in a frying pan and cook the pine nuts until golden brown. Spoon the hot butter and pine nuts over the fatteh and serve.

Kousa bi laban is a very simple name. *Kousa* means 'zucchini' (courgette) and *laban* means 'yoghurt'. In the Middle East, this is a very popular dish. The zucchini are filled with a delicious spicy meat and rice mixture, which goes perfectly with the creamy sauce. Once when we were making this dish, our very fun and enthusiastic Syrian friend Ghania arrived unexpectedly. She saw the zucchini and, without asking, she immediately started to transform our dish into the kousa bi laban that they make in her home city of Homs, which is very different from the Lebanese version. This is why we love our Middle Eastern ladies.

Kousa bi laban

LEBANESE-STYLE AND SYRIAN-STYLE FROM HOMS

— Cut each zucchini into thirds, then hollow out each piece with an apple corer. Do not hollow all the way through — one end should remain closed.

— Combine the rice, lamb and onion, using your hands to mix it all up. Add a sprinkling of seven spice, cinnamon, a little nutmeg and some black pepper to season. Fill the hollowed zucchini pieces with the rice mixture about three-quarters of the way (not quite full because the rice will expand). Stand the zucchini pieces in a saucepan and fill part of the way up with water. Cover and cook for 15–20 minutes, until the zucchini is tender. Drain.

— Mix the cornflour with a little cold water to make a paste. Place the yoghurt in large, deep frying pan over medium heat and mix with the cornflour paste and some salt and sumac. Bring to a simmer and place the stuffed zucchini into the sauce. Sprinkle with the chopped mint or parsley and some more sumac.

— For the Homs version, after hollowing out the zucchini, heat a generous amount of olive oil in a pan and fry the zucchini pieces until golden brown. Let them cool down. Fill the fried zucchini with the stuffing as above; you won't have to cook the zucchini in the water for as long.

— Serves 4–6

4–6 SMALL LIGHT GREEN
  ZUCCHINI (COURGETTES)
200 G (7 OZ) RICE
200 G (7 OZ) MINCED (GROUND) LAMB
1 ONION *finely chopped*
SEVEN SPICE
GROUND CINNAMON
GROUND NUTMEG
BLACK PEPPER
1½ TABLESPOONS CORNFLOUR
  (CORN STARCH)
750 G (1 LB 11 OZ/3 CUPS) FULL-FAT
  ORGANIC YOGHURT
SALT
SUMAC
A FEW MINT OR PARSLEY SPRIGS
  leaves finely chopped
OLIVE OIL

Slow-cooked lamb

WITH MASTIC, TOMATO, CINNAMON AND ROSEWATER

— *Serves 4–6*

4 ONIONS *sliced*

4 GARLIC CLOVES *finely chopped*

3 LARGE TOMATOES *finely chopped*

500 G (1 LB 2 OZ) BONELESS LAMB LEG
   cut into chunks

OLIVE OIL

2 CINNAMON OR CASSIA STICKS

2 TEASPOONS MASTIC
   *finely ground in a mortar
   (mastic is available from European
   or Middle Eastern grocers)*

SALT

ROSEWATER

DRIED ROSE PETALS

Mastic is a resinous gum from the mastic tree, rarely seen outside of Greek and Arabic cooking. It has a very unique flavour and is most often used in ice cream and baked sweets. It's a special addition here with the lamb; it imparts a really special flavour and gives the sauce a beautiful, slightly milky colour. Combined with rose petals and cinnamon, it's really delicious. Serve on the mezze table in small portions.

— In a heavy-based saucepan or cast-iron casserole, fry the onion, garlic, tomato and lamb in a large spoonful of olive oil for 10 minutes over low heat. Add the cinnamon or cassia, the mastic and enough water to almost cover the meat. Add salt and simmer gently, partially covered, over low heat for 2–3 hours. At the end of cooking, add a little dash of rosewater and scatter with rose petals.

The grill

The grill is very popular in mezze-land and always comes after all other mezze dishes. Usually there's not a lot of choice (just chicken or red meat), but we are glad to bring you some variety – from fish and shellfish to meat and poultry, and even flatbread. We love the grill, and it's also a real Mediterranean way of cooking. If you have no barbecue at your disposal, or if it's too cold to cook outside, then you can just use a griddle pan or grill (broiler). We like to encourage improvisation!

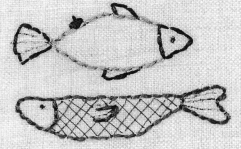

Our samke harra

— *Serves 4–6*

5 GARLIC CLOVES

TURKISH RED PEPPER FLAKES
   (pul biber or Aleppo pepper)

OLIVE OIL

1 LARGE DORY OR SEA BASS
   or other big tasty fish

SALT

6 LARGE TOMATOES

3 RED CHILLIES

1 BUNCH CORIANDER (CILANTRO)
   coarsely chopped

Samke harra is hot fish (*samke* means 'fish' and *harra* means 'hot'). The classic version is made with hot pepper and tahini sauce, but this is our take on the dish. The sauce is ridiculous easy. You mix the ingredients — tomatoes, chillies and garlic — cook them down and then add oil, water and coriander (cilantro). So simple.

— Preheat a barbecue grill to high, or the oven to 200°C (400°F).

— Crush two of the garlic cloves with a sprinkling of red pepper flakes and a large slug of olive oil. Rub all over the fish and sprinkle with salt. Grill the fish for 15–20 minutes, depending on its size, until cooked and light golden brown. Baste occasionally with any remaining garlic oil.

— Meanwhile, place the remaining garlic, the tomatoes and chillies in a dry heavy-based saucepan over medium–high heat. Leave everything whole. Cover with the lid and cook until the tomatoes and peppers are puffed and browned (but not burned). Add a large spoon of oil, along with some water and salt. Allow the sauce to cook down for 10–15 minutes.

— Roughly blend the sauce, so that some texture still remains. Stir in the coriander and season to taste if needed. Spoon some of the sauce onto the fish and serve the remainder in a bowl for the table.

Grilled flatbreads
WITH POMEGRANATE MOLASSES-STEWED LAMB

— *Serves 4–8*

4 GARLIC CLOVES

1 ONION

OLIVE OIL

400 G (14 OZ) BONELESS LAMB LEG

POMEGRANATE MOLASSES

SALT

TURKISH RED PEPPER FLAKES
   (pul biber or Aleppo pepper)

FLATBREADS

TURKISH YOGHURT

MINT SPRIGS *leaves picked and chopped*

This was a revelation for us. In Amman we ate at the Syrian restaurant Naranj (famous in Damascus, and now with restaurants throughout the Middle East) and we were so impressed by this grilled flatbread stuffed with delicious braised meat. This is our attempt to replicate the dish — it may not be exactly the same, but it's still incredibly good. And super simple, as you only have to season the meat with the pomegranate molasses. It's actually our Arabic version of a pulled meat sandwich. You can also make this dish with leftover stew — just add a little pomegranate molasses.

— Finely chop the garlic and onion. Heat a large spoonful of oil in a heavy-based saucepan or cast-iron casserole and gently fry the garlic and onion over low heat. Cut the meat into pieces and add to the pan. Pour in a good slug of pomegranate molasses and enough water to almost cover the meat. Simmer gently over low heat until the meat is completely soft and falling apart, and the liquid has completely evaporated. This will take about 3–4 hours. Add extra water as needed and season with salt and red pepper flakes.

— Shred the meat using two forks. Tear the flatbreads open, fill them with the meat and drizzle with some more pomegranate molasses. Flatten the breads and cut them into small triangles. Grill on a hot griddle or in a frying pan until golden brown. Serve with some yoghurt mixed with a little pomegranate molasses and the mint leaves.

Spiced goat leg

ON THE BARBECUE

— *Serves 4–8*

8 ALLSPICE BERRIES

4 TABLESPOONS TUNISIAN BAHARAT

2 TABLESPOONS TURKISH RED
   PEPPER FLAKES
   (pul biber or Aleppo pepper)

4 TABLESPOONS CORIANDER SEEDS

3 TABLESPOONS COARSE SALT

80 ML (2½ FL OZ/⅓ CUP) MILD-
   TASTING OLIVE OIL

50 G (1¾ OZ) MELTED BUTTER

1.5 KG (3 LB 5 OZ) GOAT LEG
   with bone

Goat is a really undervalued meat. It's especially flavoursome cooked on the barbecue. The spices used here give a floral, spicy kick to this tasty piece of meat, which you definitely want to make room for after all the other mezze dishes. We do, anyway!

— Preheat the oven to 150°C (300°F). Fry the spices in a dry frying pan until fragrant, then grind them together with the salt. Mix the oil with the butter and three-quarters of the spice mix. Rub the goat well with the spice mixture and cover it tightly with foil. Place the meat on a baking tray in the middle of the oven and cook for 1½ hours. Allow to rest in the foil for about 10 minutes.

— In the meantime, prepare a coal-fired barbecue. Unwrap the goat leg and cook over the coals for about 15 minutes, until golden brown and slightly crisp. Sprinkle with the rest of the spices and serve immediately.

Shish taouk

WITH GARLIC AND SUMAC, AND POMEGRANATE, TAMARIND AND
WALNUT SAUCE

— *Serves 4—8*

6 GARLIC CLOVES

100 ML (3½ FL OZ) OLIVE OIL *plus extra*

4 TABLESPOONS SUMAC

1.3 KG (2 LB 14 OZ) ORGANIC
   WHOLE CHICKEN

SALT AND PEPPER

300 G (10½ OZ) ORGANIC SKIN-ON
   BONELESS CHICKEN THIGHS

4 TABLESPOONS TAMARIND PASTE

150 G (5½ OZ) WALNUTS *chopped*

100 ML (3½ FL OZ) POMEGRANATE
   MOLASSES

TARRAGON SPRIGS

Chicken and sumac is as classic a combination as chicken and garlic, so it's not surprising that using both combinations together results in a dish that's pretty amazing, especially with this tangy sauce made of walnuts, tart tamarind and sweet—sour pomegranate molasses.

— Preheat a grill (broiler) or barbecue grill on high.

— Peel and crush the garlic cloves and mix them with the olive oil and sumac. Butterfly the chicken, flatten it out a bit with a rolling pin and coat with two-thirds of the garlic mixture. Season with salt and pepper. Insert two metal skewers in a cross shape through the butterflied chicken to keep it in place. Rub the rest of the garlic mixture into the chicken thighs. Add some salt and pepper to season and thread the chicken thighs onto metal skewers.

— Grill the butterflied chicken for about 40 minutes, turning occasionally, until golden brown and cooked. Grill the chicken skewers for about 15 minutes, turning occasionally, until golden brown and cooked through.

— Meanwhile, make the sauce. In a small saucepan, combine the tamarind paste with 100 ml (3½ fl oz) water, the walnuts and pomegranate molasses. Bring to a simmer over low heat, then season with salt, pepper and a spoon of olive oil. Garnish the chicken with tarragon sprigs and serve alongside the sauce.

Haloumi flatbreads

WITH PARSLEY, OREGANO AND TARRAGON

— *Serves 2–4*

4–8 FLATBREADS

250 G (9 OZ) HALOUMI

SPRIGS OF PARSLEY, OREGANO
  AND TARRAGON

SPRING ONIONS (SCALLIONS)

If you, like us, have a lot of flatbread in your house, you need some creative solutions to stop it from going to waste. This recipe is a perfect example, and because it's toasted, it's a great way to use bread that isn't so fresh. It's ideal for a quick snack, a hot mezze lunch or as a bite with a beer or glass of wine before dinner.

— Tear the flatbreads in half. Cut the haloumi into strips. Divide the haloumi, herbs and spring onions among the flatbreads. Fold the flatbreads and grill them on a hot griddle or under the grill (broiler), cutting them into smaller portions to serve, if you like. So quick and so delicious.

— You could also fill the breads with labne, or use za'atar instead of the herbs.

Roasted quails

WITH STAR ANISE AND DRIED ROSE PETALS

— *Serves 4—6*

6 GARLIC CLOVES

4 STAR ANISE

4 TABLESPOONS BLACK
 PEPPERCORNS

2 TABLESPOONS ANISEED

4 TABLESPOONS SUMAC

4 TABLESPOONS DRIED ROSE PETALS

COARSE SEA SALT

4-6 ORGANIC QUAILS

125 ML (4 FL OZ/½ CUP) MILD-TASTING
 OLIVE OIL OR 100 G (3 ½ OZ)
 SOFT BUTTER

A FEW FRESH BAY LEAF SPRIGS

Blanching meats in hot broth is a cooking technique from the Far East that results in tender meat and crispy skin. We dip our quails in a brine containing the same spices as those we coat them with before grilling. Twice as good!

— Peel the garlic cloves. Crush half the garlic with half the spices in a mortar and pestle, then transfer to a saucepan with a little salt and about 1.5 litres (1½ qts) cold water. Bring to the boil over low heat and simmer for at least 1—2 hours. Check the seasoning as you go, because as the liquid boils it can become too salty; add more water if needed.

— Wash the quails and pat them dry. Bring the broth to a boil and simmer the quails, one at a time, for 2 minutes in the hot broth. Let the quails drain on a wire rack and pat them dry with paper towel.

— Crush the rest of the garlic with the remaining spices and some salt. Massage the mixture into the skin and abdominal cavities of the quails. Place, uncovered, in the fridge to dry for a minimum of 1—2 hours — the skin should begin to pull tight.

— Heat a grill (broiler) or barbecue grill on medium—high. Coat the quails with some oil or butter and grill on a bed of bay leaves for about 15 minutes, until golden brown and crisp on the outside, but still juicy inside. Serve on the fragrant bay leaves.

Pistachio kebabs

WITH DRIED ROSE PETALS, SUMAC AND BLACKENED POTATOES

— *Serves 2–4*

150 G (5½ OZ) SHELLED PISTACHIOS

SMALL HANDFUL DRIED
    ROSE PETALS

300 G (10½ OZ) MINCED
    (GROUND) LAMB

1 TABLESPOON SUMAC

SALT AND PEPPER

4 LARGE YELLOW POTATOES
    thinly sliced

We first encountered these amazing blackened potatoes when standing around a wood stove in a living room in the Lebanese mountains. The woman of the house laid the slices of potato directly on top of the stove. Sprinkled with a little salt water or fine salt, they're so crispy, smoky and nutty. And then there's the kebab ... We really love all sorts of meats, but these kebabs really take the cake. The combination of meat and pistachio is classic; just be sure to leave the nuts a little coarse.

— Using a mortar and pestle, pound the pistachios with the rose petals. Add to the minced lamb, along with the sumac and salt and pepper to season. Form the mince around some metal skewers into nice, flat, oval-shaped kebabs. Make sure to keep them flat.

— Heat a barbecue grill on high and heat a dry frying pan. Grill the kebabs on both sides until golden brown, then place the potato slices in the dry frying pan (yes, without any oil!). Cook the potato on both sides until it blackens and bubbles (this happens very quickly). Sprinkle them with a little salt water or just a little salt, and continue cooking until tender. Serve with the kebabs.

Lamb skewers
WITH CARDAMOM, TURMERIC AND GARLIC

— *Serves 4*

500 G (1 LB 2 OZ) BONELESS LAMB LEG
   OR SHOULDER

2 TEASPOONS CARDAMOM PODS

5 CM (2 IN) PIECE FRESH TURMERIC
   sliced

2 TABLESPOONS GROUND TURMERIC

3 LARGE GARLIC CLOVES

SALT

6 SHALLOTS

3–4 LEMONS

FLATBREADS

Fresh turmeric is all the rage these days, which makes it much easier to buy. We find this kind of dish ideal, because you can do all the work in advance and just grill everything up at the last moment. The taste of this marinade is explosive!

— Cut the meat into equal-sized cubes. Using a mortar and pestle, crush the cardamom pods, fresh and ground turmeric, garlic and some salt until you have a thick paste. This will take a little while, and make sure you wear an apron so that the turmeric doesn't stain your clothes. Coat the lamb with the mixture and set aside to marinate for at least 30 minutes, or ideally a few hours.

— Halve the shallots and cut the lemons into pieces. Thread the meat, lemon and shallot onto long metal skewers and grill them on a hot barbecue or under a hot grill (broiler) until golden brown on the outside but still a little pink in the middle, depending on your taste. Serve with flatbreads.

Rack of lamb

WITH LEMON AND CORIANDER RUB

— *Serves 6—8*

½ BUNCH CORIANDER (CILANTRO)

1 LEMON

2 GARLIC CLOVES

3 TABLESPOONS CORIANDER SEEDS

1 TABLESPOON BLACK PEPPERCORNS

SALT

2 LAMB RACKS *about 2 kg (4 lb 6 oz)*
   in total

MILD-TASTING OLIVE OIL

If you divide a lamb rack into portions, you get lamb cutlets. We left the lamb rack whole in this dish, but of course individual cutlets work great, too.

— Roughly chop the coriander, grate the zest of the lemon and peel the garlic. Crush to a paste in a mortar and pestle, along with the coriander seeds, peppercorns and a little salt. Coat the lamb racks with three-quarters of the paste, reserving the rest for serving. Place in the fridge for a minimum of 30 minutes to marinate, then remove before cooking and allow to come to room temperature.

— Preheat a barbecue grill to high. Coat the lamb racks generously with oil, then roast on the barbecue (with the lid closed) for 20—30 minutes, until golden brown on the outside but still pink inside. Cover the lamb with foil and allow to rest for 10 minutes before carving. Combine the reserved marinade with a little olive oil and serve alongside the meat.

Stuffed eggplant

WITH BULGHUR, WALNUTS AND MINT

— *Serves 4–6*

2 WHITE ONIONS

75 G (2¾ OZ) WALNUTS

½ BUNCH FRESH MINT
  leaves picked, plus extra to serve

100 G (3½ OZ) FINE BULGHUR

65 G (2¼ OZ) TOMATO PASTE

1 TABLESPOON DRIED MINT

1–2 TEASPOONS TURKISH RED
  PEPPER FLAKES
  (pul biber or Aleppo pepper)

SALT

MILD-TASTING OLIVE OIL

3 FIRM EGGPLANTS (AUBERGINES)

TURKISH YOGHURT

We say it often, but this is another dish where you will definitely not miss the meat. This dish makes a fantastic centrepiece to a meatless mezze table ...

— Chop the onions, walnuts and mint leaves very finely and combine in a bowl with the bulghur, tomato paste, dried mint, red pepper flakes and salt to taste. Mix in a large spoonful of olive oil.

— Preheat the oven to the highest setting. Cut the eggplants in half lengthways and scoop out some of the flesh (keep it for soup or a dip). Place the eggplants on a baking tray and fill them with the bulghur mixture. Drizzle with some oil and sprinkle with a little more salt and red pepper. Cook the eggplants in the middle of the hot oven until golden brown and cooked through.

— Serve drizzled with olive oil and sprinkled with some fresh mint leaves, and with some creamy yoghurt on the side.

Grilled clams

WITH GARLIC OIL, SUMAC, PRESERVED LEMON
AND PARSLEY

— *Serves 2–4*

1 SMALL BUNCH PARSLEY
  coarsely chopped
200 ML (7 FL OZ) GOOD-QUALITY
  OLIVE OIL
1 TABLESPOON SUMAC
½ PRESERVED LEMON
  peel only, finely chopped
1 GARLIC CLOVE
SALT
1 KG (2 LB 3 OZ) CLAMS
  or other delicious shellfish, cleaned
BREAD

We wanted to do something with shellfish for this book. Then the thought struck us: what if we just throw them on the grill with some nice oil, sumac and preserved lemon? And it was delicious! We (that is us, our stylist Maaike and Ernie the photographer) celebrated by devouring the clams you see in the photo within moments. Mop up all the delicious sauce with bread.

— Make the garlic oil by blending the parsley, olive oil, sumac, preserved lemon and garlic with a stick blender. Season with salt, but be careful as the preserved lemon is also salty.

— Heat a barbecue grill plate to hot and tip the clams onto the plate. When the clams open, drizzle them generously with the garlic oil. Eat them right away with your fingers and some bread. You can also make this dish using a hot frying pan!

Pumpkin kibbeh

WITH SPINACH, LABNE AND POMEGRANATE MOLASSES

— *Serves 6—8*

SEA SALT

300 G (10½ OZ) TURKISH YOGHURT

300 G (10½ OZ) PUMPKIN (WINTER SQUASH) *skin on, seeds removed*

8 ONIONS

OLIVE OIL

300 G (10½ OZ) WILD SPINACH

300 G (10½ OZ) FINE BULGHUR

150 G (5½ OZ) PINE NUTS

1 TABLESPOON SUMAC

2-3 TABLESPOONS POMEGRANATE MOLASSES

Pumpkin (winter squash) kibbeh and potato kibbeh are traditionally made during periods in which no meat may be eaten, such as the fasting season for Easter. This dish, then, is for everyone. The combination of the pumpkin, onions and pomegranate molasses in this interpretation of a classic is a really good one.

— Stir a little salt through the yoghurt. Place a square of clean muslin (cheesecloth) on a work surface and spoon the yoghurt on top. Tie up the corners to create a bag, then transfer to a colander set over a bowl or saucepan. Place in the fridge and leave for at least 4 hours to make soft labne.

— Preheat the oven to 200°C (400°F). Cut the pumpkin into pieces and bake until soft and cooked through.

— Halve the onions, slice them thinly and fry in a large spoonful of oil over medium heat for about 30 minutes, until golden brown. Season with salt. Fry the spinach in a frying pan over high heat until wilted. Drain.

— Scoop the pumpkin flesh from the peel, mash gently and mix with the bulghur and a little salt to make a firm dough. Divide the mixture into two, with one portion slightly larger than the other. Press the smaller piece into a flat circle or rectangle in a baking dish or on a baking tray. Spoon the spinach on top, along with the labne, pine nuts and onion. Sprinkle generously with sumac and pomegranate molasses. Using the remaining dough, make another, slightly larger circle or rectangle. Place it over the filling and press the edges together. Drizzle with plenty of olive oil and bake the kibbeh under the grill (broiler) for 15—20 minutes, until golden brown and cooked. Cut into rectangles or diamonds and serve.

A tip from a Moroccan mama: to stuff a chicken, carve down the backbone with a sharp knife; this allows you to 'break' the chicken creating more space. Fill the abdominal cavity and close everything up by tying the legs together with kitchen twine. If you still can't fit all the stuffing in, just place in a roasting tin under the chicken and cook it together with the meat.

Stuffed saffron chicken
WITH BARBERRY AND DILL RICE AND ADVIEH

— *Serves about 4*

100 G (3½ OZ) ARBORIO RICE

150 G (5½ OZ) SOFT BUTTER

4 TABLESPOONS ADVIEH
  (*Iranian spice blend; available from
  Middle Eastern grocers*)

2 PINCHES SAFFRON STRANDS

SALT AND PEPPER

1.2 KG (2 LB 10 OZ) WHOLE ORGANIC
  CHICKEN

1 BUNCH DILL

2 TABLESPOONS BARBERRIES

80 ML (2½ FL OZ/⅓ CUP) MILD-
  TASTING OLIVE OIL

— Soak the rice for a minimum of 30 minutes in some cold water. Preheat the oven to its maximum temperature.

— Mix the butter with 2 tablespoons of the advieh, the saffron and some salt and pepper. Rub the butter mixture under the skin of the chicken, being careful not to tear it. Rub any remaining butter on the outside and in the cavity of the chicken.

— Rinse the rice until the water runs clear. Drain well. Finely chop the dill and add to the rice along with the barberries, some salt and pepper and the olive oil. Stuff the chicken with the rice and place in a greased roasting tin. Place the dish in the middle of the hot oven and reduce the temperature to 170°C. Roast for about 1 hour, until golden brown and cooked through. Allow to rest for about 10 minutes before serving.

Man'ouche

WITH KASHK, GARLIC OIL AND SESAME SEEDS

— *Serves 2–4*

1 QUANTITY LABNE BALLS
   (see page 82)

2 TEASPOONS DRIED YEAST

500 G (1 LB 2 OZ) FLOUR

SALT FLAKES

2 GARLIC CLOVES

OLIVE OIL

2 TABLESPOONS SESAME SEEDS

NIGELLA SEEDS

Kashk is truly a must for lovers of fermented food. It can be made from bulghur or labne. For the bulghur version, the grain is mixed with water and allowed to ferment for a few days. The sour bulghur is then pressed, dried and ground to a powder that has a fresh, sour taste. For the labne version, which is what we've made here, labne is left to ripen and dry out. Kashk is eaten in Lebanon's mountains as a rustic winter soup: made with water and cured meat. I love it, but Nadia is not really a fan at all. It can be an acquired taste!

— Leave the labne balls at room temperature for 2–3 days. This will be the kashk.

— Mix the yeast with a little lukewarm water and set aside until frothy. Mix with the flour, salt and enough lukewarm water to make a cohesive dough. Knead the dough for about 15 minutes and then cover it and place in a warm spot to rise.

— Slice the garlic and fry in a little oil until golden. Mix the kashk with some oil.

— Divide the dough into portions and roll them out on a clean work surface. Cook the flatbreads on a barbecue hotplate, in a hot frying pan or under a hot grill (broiler). Spread the flatbreads with the kashk. Mix the sesame seeds with the olive oil and garlic and drizzle over the top of the kashk. Finish with a sprinkle of salt flakes and nigella seeds.

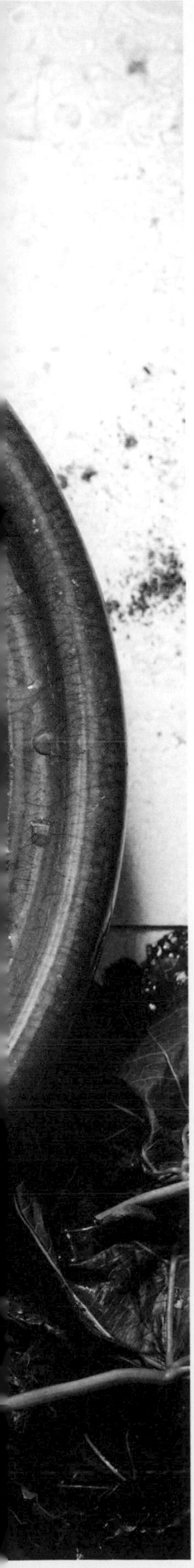

Dory in vine leaves

WITH SEVEN SPICE

— *Serves 4*

2 × 500 G (1 LB 2 OZ) DORY *cleaned*

3 TABLESPOONS SEVEN SPICE

SALT

8–12 VINE LEAVES *fresh or dried*

EXTRA-VIRGIN OLIVE OIL

The vine leaves serve as a kind of protective layer to keep the aromas and flavours inside the fish, so the dory remains deliciously juicy.

— Heat a grill (broiler) or barbecue grill on high. Score the fish with a sharp knife and sprinkle generously with seven spice and salt. Place the fish on a baking tray and wrap well with vine leaves. Drizzle with some oil and cook for 20–30 minutes (depending on the size of the fish), until cooked through and crisp. Serve sprinkled with salt and olive oil.

Grilled trout
WITH SUMAC AND GARLIC OIL

— *Serves 2 (or more)*

4–8 TROUT *cleaned*

SALT

3 GARLIC CLOVES

4 TABLESPOONS SUMAC

100 ML (3½ FL OZ) EXTRA-VIRGIN
 OLIVE OIL

ABOUT 60 ML (2 FL OZ/¼ CUP)
 LEMON JUICE

We've never been big fans of trout or freshwater fish in general, until we tried this combination of tangy sumac and raw (tasty!) garlic. So delicious.

— Heat a barbecue grill or a griddle pan over high heat. Wash the trout and pat dry with paper towel. Sprinkle the fish with plenty of salt. Peel and grate the garlic cloves, then mix with the sumac, olive oil, lemon juice and some salt. Grill the fish until golden brown and cooked through — about 12 minutes, depending on the size of the fish. Serve with the sumac–garlic oil.

Iraqi kebab
WITH SUMAC AND SALT

— *Serves 2—4*

400 G (14 OZ) MINCED (GROUND)
   FATTY LAMB
COARSE SALT
SUMAC

Iraqis love their kebabs to be rich, with a lot of fat in the meat. It's not how we would usually eat our kebabs, but it is certainly delicious, so we encourage you to try it out! The most important thing here is that you ask your butcher for minced (ground) lamb — or even better, minced sheep or mutton — with a lot of fat. The tartness of the sumac is a perfect complement to the fatty meat.

— Knead the mince with some salt. Form the mince around long metal skewers, flattening the meat out a little.

— Grill the kebabs on a barbecue grill on high or under a grill (broiler). Cook until golden brown and cooked through. Serve sprinkled with plenty of sumac and some salt.

Chicken kebab
WITH GRILLED SPRING ONIONS

— *Serves 2–4*

100 G (3½ OZ) ALMONDS

100 G (3½ OZ) SHELLED PISTACHIOS

400 G (14 OZ) SKIN-ON BONELESS
   CHICKEN THIGHS

2 GARLIC CLOVES

SALT

TURKISH RED PEPPER FLAKES
   (*pul biber or Aleppo pepper*)

1 SMALL BUNCH SPRING ONIONS
   (SCALLIONS)

Chicken kebabs aren't traditional, but that's never stopped us before! The added nuts make the dish exciting, and using spring onions (scallions) instead of skewers is fun and, most importantly, tasty.

— Chop the nuts in a food processor. Add the chicken and garlic and season with salt and red pepper flakes. Process until well combined, then shape kebabs around the spring onions. Grill the kebabs on a hot barbecue grill or in a hot oven, until cooked and golden brown. Serve immediately.

After dinner

Sweets are very beautiful and elegant
in the Arab world, but after dinner, you
usually eat just a little fruit as a snack.
Something more sophisticated, such as
osmalieh or baklava, would be eaten in the
afternoon. However, we are happy to eat
sweets at any time of day, even dessert.

An after-dinner coffee or hot water
with orange-blossom water is a perfect
digestive, if you wish to make room for
dessert after a big meal — we speak from
extensive experience!

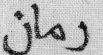

Arabic coffee

— *Makes 4 small coffees*

1–2 TABLESPOONS SUGAR

2 TABLESPOONS ARABIC COFFEE

Good Arabic coffee takes a little care to prepare, but it couldn't be more simple. For a great digestive, you can make 'white' coffee, which is just adding a few drops of orange-blossom water (for beginners) or a proper splash (for the advanced) to boiling water. And if you have fresh or dried orange blossom, you can of course add that too. Arabic coffee is an extra-fine grind, with or without *hil* (cardamom) added. You'll find Arabic coffee at Turkish, Moroccan and Middle Eastern grocers.

— Bring 200 ml (7 fl oz) water with 1–2 tablespoons of sugar to the boil in a raqwa (Arabic coffee pot) or in a saucepan. Add 2 full tablespoons of Arabic coffee and bring to the boil. Lift the pan from the heat as soon as the water is boiling, wait for the boil to die down, and then lower the coffee pot over the heat again. This is repeated a total of three times.

— Carefully spoon or pour hot coffee into small Arabic or espresso cups and let it stand so that the coffee can settle. And for the soothsayers among us: once you have finished your drink, place the saucer on top of the empty coffee cup and tip it over. Remove the cup and read the future in the grinds ... yalla!

Mahleb pudding

— *Serves 4*

1 TEASPOON MAHLEB

750 ML (25½ FL OZ/3 CUPS)
  UNSWEETENED ALMOND MILK

2–3 TABLESPOONS SUGAR

1 EGG YOLK

2 TABLESPOONS CORNFLOUR
  (CORN STARCH)

SALT

4 TABLESPOONS NUTS (*such as
  pistachios and/or hazelnuts*)

Mahleb are the pits of a certain type of cherry. The flavour is somewhere between bitter almond, apricot and cherry. You either love it or hate it.

— Tie the mahleb up in a piece of clean muslin (cheesecloth), place in a saucepan with the almond milk and sugar, and bring to the boil over medium heat.

— Combine the egg yolk and cornflour with a spoonful of cold water or almond milk. Add to the saucepan with a pinch of salt and stir until the mixture thickens. Pour the pudding into serving dishes and allow to cool and set. Chop the nuts and sprinkle over the pudding just before serving.

Sour cherry and olive oil sorbet

WITH ROSEWATER

— *Serves 6–8*

1 LITRE (1 QT) SOUR CHERRY JUICE

50 ML (1¾ FL OZ) EXTRA-VIRGIN
   OLIVE OIL

ROSEWATER

HONEY *if needed*

Fragrant olive oil and rosewater combine with cherry juice to make a surprisingly creamy sorbet. An ice-cream machine is the easiest way to make this, but if you don't have one, you can freeze it in an airtight container. Two hours before serving, allow the mixture to sit at room temperature for 15 minutes then purée with a stick blender until smooth and creamy. Return to the freezer.

— Whisk the cherry juice with the oil and some rosewater to taste. The sweetness and flavours should be quite strong, as freezing will make the taste less pronounced. If the mixture isn't sweet enough, add some honey. Churn the mixture in an ice-cream machine according to the manufacturer's instructions, or use the freezer method we described above.

Osmalieh is very classic and very, very beautiful. What's more, it's not difficult to make! In fact, it's extremely simple — and everyone will *ooh* and *ahh* over the result. It's a wonderful example of how elegant and enchanting Arabic sweets can be.

The filling is a kind of dairy cream called *ashta*. Ashta is hard to find, so a mix of cottage cheese, ricotta and mascarpone comes very close. The kataifi pastry looks like angel-hair pasta, and is usually found in the freezer at Turkish or Middle Eastern grocers. Use baking rings if you have them, but egg rings or rings made from foil will also do.

Osmalieh

WITH PISTACHIOS AND ORANGE-BLOSSOM SYRUP

⅓ PACKET KATAIFI PASTRY
defrosted

75 G (2¾ OZ) BUTTER *melted*

200 G (7 OZ) SUGAR *plus extra*

ANISEED

ORANGE-BLOSSOM WATER

200 G (7 OZ) COTTAGE CHEESE

200 G (7 OZ) RICOTTA

200 G (7 OZ) MASCARPONE

75 G (2¾ OZ) SHELLED GREEN
PISTACHIOS *of the highest quality*

— Preheat the oven to 180°C (350°F). Place the pastry in a wide bowl with the melted butter, a little sugar to taste and 1 tablespoon of aniseed. Mix well.

— Combine the 200 g (7 oz) of sugar in a saucepan with 200 ml (7 fl oz) water and simmer over low heat for 15–20 minutes, until reduced to a syrup. Sprinkle with a large spoonful of orange-blossom water (to taste, of course — we love it, so we like to add a lot, but if you're unfamiliar with the flavour, start with just a little). Transfer to a serving jug.

— To make the filling, stir the cottage cheese, ricotta and mascarpone together. Finely chop the pistachios.

— Line a baking tray with baking paper and place a baking ring on it. Fill the ring with a handful of kataifi and press it down carefully to make a round. Remove the ring and repeat this procedure until you have eight rounds of pastry. Bake until golden brown. This can be very quick, depending on your oven, so keep your eye on it!

— Place four kataifi rounds onto serving plates. Cover with a layer of creamy filling and top with the remaining rounds, taking care as the pastry is very fragile. Sprinkle the osmalieh with the crushed pistachios and let everyone pour their own orange-blossom syrup over the top.

Salep is a powder made from orchid root. The Ottomans drank salep for a long time before they embraced tea and coffee, and it's still widely drunk in Turkey and Greece, where it's used to make a comforting hot drink in winter. Here, we turn milky salep into a decadent ice cream, flavoured with thyme. This makes a perfect dessert.

Salep and thyme ice cream

WITH KATAIFI AND HONEY

— *Serves 4–6*

400 ML (13½ FL OZ) MILK

5 TABLESPOONS SALEP POWDER
*(available from Turkish or
Middle Eastern grocers)*

2 FRESH THYME SPRIGS

75 G (2¾ OZ) BUTTER

¼ PACKET FROZEN KATAIFI PASTRY
defrosted

4–6 TABLESPOONS HONEY

— Combine the milk, salep powder and thyme sprigs in a saucepan and heat very gently for about 30 minutes. Set aside to cool. Remove the thyme sprigs and churn the mixture in an ice-cream machine according to the manufacturer's instructions, or pour it into a sealable plastic container and freeze for 3–4 hours, stirring the mixture every 30 minutes with a wooden spoon,

— Heat the oven to 200°C (400°F). Melt the butter in a saucepan and mix through the kataifi. Add some honey to taste. Spread the kataifi onto a baking tray lined with baking paper and bake in the middle of the oven for about 8 minutes, until golden.

— Serve a scoop of salep ice cream on some crisp kataifi and drizzle with honey. Serve immediately.

This cake is inspired by sweets we have eaten in pastry shops during our travels, such as the famous Hallab in Tripoli, Lebanon. There is a reason people like to go there with an empty stomach: the range of pastries, baklava and ice creams is extraordinary and everything is mouth-watering. If you want to eat Arabic sweets as dessert, we recommend that you take small portions. Not because they don't taste good, but because they are generally very rich.

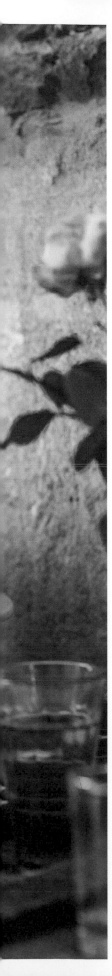

Pistachio and semolina cake

WITH MERINGUE

— *Serves about 20*

2 EGGS

150 ML (5 FL OZ) PEANUT OIL

150 G (5½ OZ) YOGHURT

150 G (5½ OZ) LIGHT BROWN
   SUGAR

SALT

300 G (10½ OZ) FINE SEMOLINA
   plus extra

150 G (5½ OZ) COARSE SEMOLINA

1 TEASPOON BAKING POWDER

1 TABLESPOON BICARB SODA
   (BAKING SODA)

230 G (8 OZ) SUGAR

2 TABLESPOONS LEMON JUICE

1 TABLESPOON ORANGE-BLOSSOM
   WATER

2 EGG WHITES

1 TABLESPOON CORNFLOUR
   (CORN STARCH)

400 G (14 OZ) SHELLED
   PISTACHIOS

150 G (5½ OZ) ICING
   (CONFECTIONERS') SUGAR

1 EGG YOLK

2-3 TABLESPOONS PISTACHIO OIL

— Heat the oven to 160°C (320°F). Grease two 24 cm (9½ in) cake tins and dust them lightly with semolina.

— In a stand mixer, beat the eggs with the peanut oil, yoghurt, sugar and ½ teaspoon of salt until thick and creamy. Fold both types of semolina through the mixture using a wooden spoon. Add the baking powder and bicarb soda little by little, stirring to combine. Divide the batter between the cake tins and bake in the middle of the oven for about 45 minutes, until cooked through and golden brown. Let the cakes cool in the tins, then turn out onto a wire rack and allow to cool completely.

— In a saucepan, combine 200 g (7 oz) of sugar with the lemon juice, orange-blossom water and 60 ml (2 fl oz/¼ cup) water. Bring to a gentle simmer. Place a sugar thermometer in the pan.

— When the sugar thermometer reaches 113°C (235°F), start beating the egg whites in a clean stand-mixer bowl. Add the remaining 30 g (1 oz) of sugar and the cornflour. Beat until the egg white is the consistency of thick yoghurt. When the sugar thermometer reaches 118°C (244°F), add the sugar syrup to the meringue in a thin, steady stream, and keep beating on high speed until you have stiff shiny peaks.

— Grind the pistachios in a food processor. Set 2 tablespoons of the pistachios aside for decoration. Keep the remainder in the food processor and add the icing sugar, a pinch of salt and the egg yolk. Blend to a smooth, firm paste. Roll the pistachio paste between two sheets of baking paper to make a 24 cm (9½ in) circle.

— Place one of the cakes on a stand or serving plate. Cover with the pistachio paste and top with the second cake. Spoon the meringue on top, sprinkle with the remaining pistachio powder and drizzle with the pistachio oil.

Filo triangles
WITH MOZZARELLA AND CUMQUATS

— *Makes 12 triangles*

75 G (2¾ OZ) SUGAR

ORANGE-BLOSSOM WATER

100 G (3½ OZ) FRESH CUMQUATS

1 BALL FRESH MOZZARELLA

2 LARGE SHEETS FILO PASTRY

1 EGG YOLK *lightly beaten*

OIL *for frying*

We made these quick baklava-like pastry triangles with mozzarella and cumquats because that's what we had in the fridge at the time. If you don't have any cumquats, these are just as delicious made with lemon, orange, grapefruit or lime. And even if you don't have any mozzarella, that's no problem, because haloumi, feta or ricotta are just as tasty. As you can see, the variations and combinations are endless.

— In a saucepan, combine the sugar with 75 ml (2½ fl oz) water and a few drops of orange-blossom water. Bring to the boil. Slice the cumquats and set 2 tablespoons aside for the filling. Add the rest to the sugar syrup and gently simmer.

— Cut the mozzarella into small pieces and mix with the reserved cumquat. Cut each sheet of filo pastry into six long strips. Lay out a strip in front of you and cover the rest of the pastry with a clean, damp tea towel. In one corner of the pastry strip, place a spoonful of the filling. Fold the other corner over the filling to make a triangle, and then fold the triangle over. Keep folding until you reach the end of the pastry. Seal the pastry with some egg and make the rest of the triangles in the same way.

— Heat a large layer of oil in a wok and fry the triangles for a few seconds on each side, until golden brown. Drain on paper towel. Place the triangles on a wire rack and drizzle with the hot sugar syrup. Allow to cool and crisp up before eating.

Often, classic mezze restaurants will serve fresh fruit for dessert, accompanied with a selection of candied fruits and vegetables, such as pumpkin (winter squash), eggplant (aubergine) and carrot.

To make the classic Arabic sugar syrup *attar* or *qattar*, simmer 200 g (7 oz) of sugar with 200 ml (7 fl oz) water, a spoon of lemon juice, and orange-blossom water and/or rosewater to taste, then reduce down to a fairly thick, transparent syrup. You can store it for a long time in the fridge. Use firm, not-too-sweet dates for the best results. Of course, you can drink Arabic or white coffee with this dish — but have you ever thought of making your own herbal tea? Try a blend of lemongrass, citrus peel, cardamom, fresh ginger, rose buds and other dried flowers, along with dried apples. It's a lovely refreshment to serve with sweets.

Candied dates

WITH CARDAMOM, GINGER AND DRIED ROSES

— *Makes 250 g (9 oz)*

5 CM (2 IN) PIECE GINGER

3 CARDAMOM PODS

1 TABLESPOON DRIED ROSE
   PETALS AND BUDS

250 G (9 OZ) PITTED DATES

200 ML (7 FL OZ) CLASSIC SUGAR
   SYRUP *(see opposite)*

— Peel and coarsely grate the ginger. Lightly crush the cardamom pods and rose petals and buds.

— In a saucepan over low heat, combine the dates with the ginger, cardamom, rose petals and buds, sugar syrup and a splash of water. Simmer gently for at least 30 minutes. If the syrup starts to boil dry, add a splash of water. Set aside to cool, then serve.

Muhallabia

WITH ROASTED WALNUTS AND MANDARIN SUGAR

— *Serves 6—8*

1 LITRE (1 QT) FULL-FAT (WHOLE) MILK

75 G (2¾ OZ) SUGAR

30 G (1 OZ) CORNFLOUR
(CORN STARCH)

1 SACHET MASTIC
*finely crushed (available from
European or Middle Eastern grocers)*

ORANGE-BLOSSOM WATER

75 G (2¾ OZ) WALNUTS

GRATED ZEST OF 1 MANDARIN

Muhallabia is the Middle Eastern version of custard. If you have any left over, it makes a delicious filling for filo or puff pastry!

— Heat the milk and 50 g (1¾ oz) of the sugar in a heavy-based saucepan over low heat. Stir until the sugar is dissolved. In a separate bowl, combine the cornflour with enough cold water to make a smooth paste. Add to the milk and stir with a wooden spoon until the custard starts to simmer in the middle of the pan and the mixture coats the back of the spoon. Stir in the mastic and a few drops of orange-blossom water. Strain the muhallabia into a bowl and keep stirring until it is cooled and thickened. Set aside in a cool place (but not in the fridge).

— Roast the walnuts in a dry frying pan until lightly browned and fragrant. Roughly chop, then mix with the mandarin zest and the remaining sugar. Sprinkle on top of the muhallabia just before serving.

Rice pudding

WITH TURMERIC, TAHINI AND PINE NUTS

— *Serves 4—6*

150 G (5½ OZ) SHORT-GRAIN RICE

2 TABLESPOONS GROUND TURMERIC

3 CM (1¼ IN) PIECE FRESH TURMERIC

1 ORANGE

200 ML (7 FL OZ) MILK

50 G (1¾ OZ) SUGAR *plus extra*

100 G (3½ OZ) PINE NUTS

100 ML (3½ FL OZ) TAHINI

200 G (7 OZ) MASCARPONE

This recipe is based on moufataka, a golden rice pudding from Beirut, which our friend Mazen introduced us to. It was a dish we were unfamiliar with, but we've done our best to recreate it here. You'll need to start this recipe one day in advance.

— Place the rice in a heavy-based saucepan with 300 ml (10 fl oz) cold water and the ground turmeric. Leave to soak overnight.

— Peel and slice the fresh turmeric. Zest and juice the orange. Place the saucepan with the rice over medium heat and bring to the boil. Add the milk, 1 teaspoon of the orange zest, the fresh turmeric and the sugar. Reduce the heat to low and simmer gently, stirring often, for about 12 minutes.

— Combine three-quarters of the pine nuts with the tahini and blend with a stick blender. Stir into the rice, then spoon the pudding into serving glasses. Toast the remainder of the pine nuts in a dry frying pan with a little sugar until golden brown. Tip onto a plate to cool and crisp up. Combine the mascarpone with the orange juice and remaining zest, then spoon onto the puddings and top with the pine nuts. Serve with small spoons.

This classic fruit dessert varies depending on the season. This isn't really a recipe, but colourful seasonal fruit, displayed abundantly in gorgeous bowls or on stands, should always steal the show. In summer, fruit bowls are filled with melons of all kinds and sizes, and in winter it's all about citrus. See what's available and delicious; fruit that is in season always tastes the best. The almonds can, of course, be replaced with any other nuts. This is also a good way to use nuts that have been sitting around in your pantry for a while — the roasting and the spices will freshen their texture and flavour.

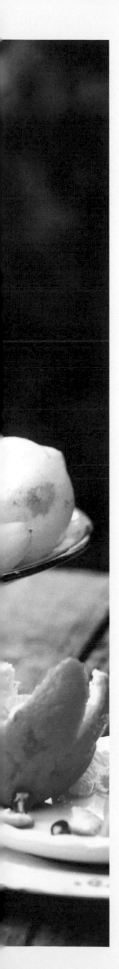

Fruit bowl
WITH ROASTED ALLSPICE ALMONDS

— *Serves as many as you like*

SEASONAL FRUIT

6 ALLSPICE BERRIES

200 G (7 OZ) ALMONDS

COARSE SALT

— Arrange your fruit in a lovely bowl or on a platter.

— Crush the allspice using a mortar and pestle. Toast the almonds in a dry frying pan. Sprinkle them with a little salt and water, and cook a little longer. Sprinkle with the allspice and some more salt, and allow to cool completely before serving with the fruit.

Buttery date and sesame cookies

— *Makes about 20*

300 G (10½ OZ) SOFT PITTED DATES

100 G (3½ OZ) BUTTER, SOFTENED

60 ML (2 FL OZ/¼ CUP) DATE SYRUP

SALT

1 EGG YOLK

200 G (7 OZ) SELF-RAISING FLOUR

200 G (7 OZ) SESAME SEEDS

50 G (1¾ OZ) SUGAR

ORANGE-BLOSSOM WATER

ICING (CONFECTIONERS') SUGAR
  (optional)

This is our fusion of classic Moroccan date cookies and Middle Eastern ma'amoul cookies. The dates give the cookies a lovely caramel colour and sweet flavour, while the filling is made of nutty sesame.

— Purée the dates into a smooth paste. Add the butter, date syrup, a pinch of salt and the egg yolk, and mix to combine. Quickly knead in the flour to make a soft, cohesive dough. Cover and place in the fridge.

— Crush half of the sesame seeds and combine with the sugar and a spoon of orange-blossom water. Mix in the rest of the sesame seeds.

— Preheat the oven to 150°C (300°F). Line a baking tray with baking paper. Divide the date mixture into about 20 balls. Flatten each date ball in the palm of your hand, then place some of the sesame filling in the middle and fold the dough around to enclose it. Decorate with a fork or knife tip. Place the cookies on the prepared tray and bake in the middle of the oven for about 30 minutes, until light brown and cooked. Set aside to cool, then dust with some icing sugar if you like.

Thanks

A big *shukran* and *merci ktir* to all the people who have fed us
and shared their cooking and wisdom in the creation of this
book – you are all indispensable.

Maaike – *shukran zina* for your incredible style and for bringing
our ideas to life in a real book: a book that shows who we are and
how we feel about food. Ernie – thank you for opening your home
to us and for your beautiful and laid-back photography. Kamal –
merci ktir for years of mezze indoctrination: now we always
begin with tabouleh only. And of course you have ten tabouleh
rules! Miriam and Martin – thank you for your great faith in
and enthusiasm for our love of Arabic cookbooks. Studio Jux
(studiojux.com) – thank you for lending us your beautiful dishes.
Anneke Koorman – for your beautiful embroidery! Laila Meliani
– for your nice dishes. Gerard Jansen and our colleagues at
VanillaVenture – we love that you share our passion for *SOUQ* and
that we're able to have these adventures with you. Our colleagues
at *Delicious* and *Foodies*, who support us and always follow us
feet-first into the world's ever-changing food culture. And José,
Laura, Mara and Michel – *shukran* for your kind and professional
support. *Shukran, shukran* Jose, Amale, Mariska, Nil, Muriel, Sabri,
Said and Nicolette for joining our mezze photography table! And
Nicolette, thank you for letting us use your house as an extra
photography location! Our families, who have to wait at the table
again and again, and have to do all of the dirty work: eating
everything and doing the dishes. But without your presence at
the table, there is no mezze! Thierry, Tariq and Anaroz – you are
our sweetest mezzes.

Love, Nadia and Merijn

Index

First published in 2017 by Fontaine Uitgevers
fontaineuitgevers.nl

This edition published in 2018 by Smith Street Books
Melbourne · Australia | smithstreetbooks.com

ISBN: 978-1-925418-62-0

CIP data is available from the National Library of Australia.

First edition
Text, recipes and food preparation: Nadia Zerouali and Merijn Tol
Photography: Ernie Enkler. Additional photography from the
    private collection of the authors
Creative direction and styling: Maaike Koorman
Illustrations: Maaike Koorman
Embroidery: Anneke Koorman
Graphic design: Tein Traniello
Culinary editor: Hennie Franssen-Seebregts
Editor: Akkie de Jong

This edition
Publisher: Paul McNally
Project editor: Hannah Koelmeyer, Tusk studio
Editor: Lucy Heaver, Tusk studio
Cover designer: Murray Batten

Printed and bound in China by C&C Offset Printing Co., Ltd.

Book 50
10 9 8 7 6 5 4 3 2 1